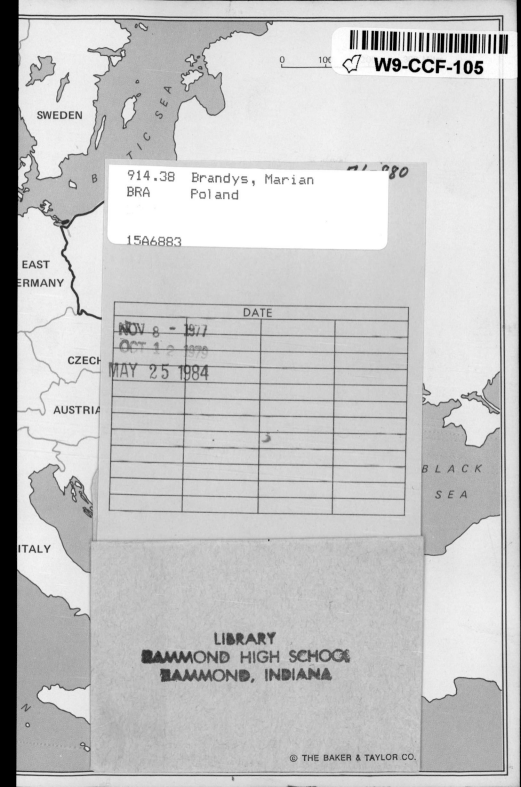

SWEDEN

EAST
GERMANY

CZECH

AUSTRIA

ITALY

BLACK
SEA

0   100

POLAND

POLAND

by Marian Brandys

photographs by Wieslaw Prazuch

DOUBLEDAY & COMPANY, INC., GARDEN CITY, NEW YORK

ISBN: 0-385-07200-7 Trade
0-385-02273-5 Prebound
Library of Congress Catalog Card Number 74–108036
Translation Copyright © 1974 by Doubleday & Company, Inc.

CONTENTS

LIST OF ILLUSTRATIONS

POLAND

Poznan International Fair

A STRANGE LAND

A POLISH JOURNALIST decided to find out what sort of impressions of Poland are taken away by foreign visitors who come to our country for various reasons and at various times of the year. He was indefatigable and accurate, so spared neither time nor labor in order to collect as much information as he could on this subject. He frequently visited airports from which long-distance Polish and foreign airplanes depart. He traveled to seaports on the Baltic, from which ships leave for the most distant places on the globe. He spent many hours at border points on international highways, where customs control of automobiles leaving Poland is carried out.

As a result of these extended efforts, the energetic journalist succeeded in carrying out a very large number of interviews with travelers of many nationalities. He talked with Americans of Polish descent who had visited with their relatives in the "old country." He talked with businessmen and industrialists who displayed their products at the International Fair in Poznan. He talked with Swedish, English and French visitors who attended the winter sports in the Tatra and Beskid mountains, or hunted duck in the Mazovian lakes or shot wild boar and deer in the Bialowieza Forest. He talked with former prisoners from Nazi concentration camps who had come to Poland for the sole purpose of seeing the places where they had suffered at Auschwitz, Treblinka and Majdanek. He talked with German tourists whose grandfathers and fathers twice occupied Poland as soldiers of Kaiser Wilhelm and Adolf Hitler; with Soviet tourists seeking the graves of sons or brothers killed in battle during World War II; with exotic students of many hues leaving Poland after completing their studies at universities in Warsaw, Cracow, Wroclaw, Danzig, Lodz, Stettin (Szczecin), Torun or Gliwice; and with many, many others too.

These interviews were very varied in content. Some people complained of the bad state of the Polish roads, of the lack of various goods in the stores, of the inadequate number of hotels and motels, of the excessive amount of formalities in doing official business of any kind, and also they complained of the very thick and fatty sauces served in Polish restaurants. Others were delighted by the charm of the Polish landscape, the magnificence of the palaces of old-time aristocrats now converted into public museums, the friendliness and hospitality of the Poles, the great changes that have occurred in various aspects of Polish life during the last twenty-five years. Yet other visitors could not get over political jokes and criticism of the government made aloud in Polish coffeehouses, and that the usual services take place in churches, attended freely by crowds of believers. The journalist also spoke with people who did not hide their disappointment at not meeting a single white bear or Soviet soldier during their stay in Poland.

But one general opinion came to the forefront in all these various interviews: "Poland is a very strange country! It is one of the strangest countries in the world!"

These very words were repeated in English, in French and German and in all the other languages our journalist understood. They were spoken in various ways: with amazement, with enthusiasm, with anger or contempt—but most often with a plain shrug of the shoulders.

Morskie Oko Lake

Is Poland really a strange country? Maybe this little book will be able to explain—in a brief, incomplete way, of course—why foreign visitors to Poland get this impression.

We must warn you in advance that our little book will not resemble the usual tourist guides. We shall not conduct our readers around all the regions of Poland, telling you in detail of the climate, landscapes, natural resources, monuments and local customs. Instead we shall try to give a bird's-eye view of the entire thousand years of the history of our country—and point out the moments which made Poland the country it is today. But this won't be a systematic guide to Polish history either. The past will be blended with the present; historical truth with legends handed down by old storytellers. We shall concentrate all our attention only on those places on the map of Poland where the most important and unusual things happened. Many other matters we shall only discuss briefly or leave out altogether.

We shall achieve our aim if our little book—despite all these oddities and faults—succeeds in interesting the reader and in arousing his liking for our country. We believe that the reader, once interested, will endeavor to widen his knowledge of Poland or will visit our country and find out for himself whether everything printed here is true. You are cordially invited. Assuredly you won't regret the trip. For centuries, Poland has been famed for hospitality. Not for nothing does one of the oldest and finest of our proverbs say: "A guest in the home means God in the home."

A LITTLE GEOGRAPHY AND HISTORY

A GLANCE AT THE MAP shows that Poland lies almost at the very center of Europe. Down the centuries, the Polish state often changed its shape and size—much more often than other states in Europe. Now it forms a more or less regular rectangle of about 312,000 square kilometers. Thus it is almost thirty times smaller than the United States and almost seventy times smaller than the Soviet Union. However, it is larger in area than Italy, Great Britain and Yugoslavia.

To the north Poland is bordered by the Baltic Sea, and to the south by the Carpathian and Sudeten mountain ranges, which separate Poland and Czechoslovakia. To the west Poland borders on the German Democratic Republic. Here two rivers mark the frontier: the Oder and its tributary the Nysa. Poland's neighbor to the east and partly also to the north is the Soviet Union. The central part of the long Polish-Soviet frontier runs along the river Bug. The three frontier rivers of Poland (the Oder, the Nysa and the Bug) have been frequently mentioned in international treaties and their names appear from time to time in the newspapers of the entire world. We shall come back to this subject later. For the time being let us consider more general matters.

Poland's geographical position has exerted through the cen-

Polish yacht on the Baltic Sea

turies a decisive influence on the shaping of its history and the personal destiny of its population. The central location of Poland in Europe has made it a natural bridge between east and west, north and south. This has brought about results of two kinds.

When relative peace prevailed in Europe, Poland played the role of an important mediator in the economic and cultural life of the entire continent, and even of the whole world. The chief trade routes led in that direction, and the influences of differing cultures crossed. These were the most advantageous years of our history. Poland grew rich, culture and learning flourished. The name of Poland was highly esteemed in world opinion.

But there were few such good and peaceful periods in Poland. More often, the "bridge" between east and west, north and south was used for purposes of war. No matter where a war broke out in Europe, sooner or later Poland became its main battlefield. The history of Poland is full of defensive wars against foreign invaders and desperate national insurrections against foreign occupants. In the Middle Ages, armies of the German Empire invaded Poland from the west, with troops of the Brandenburg and Saxon margraves, while from the north came armies of the German monastic knights, called the Knights of the Cross from the black crosses on their white cloaks. Hordes of Tartar light cavalry laid waste the territory of the Polish state in the east and south. They were the avantgarde of the powerful Mongolian empire created by Genghis Khan. To be sure, the Tartars did not occupy Polish territory permanently, but they destroyed and burned everything in their way, and when they left, took with them into slavery thousands of Polish men, women and children. Later, Poland was flooded from the north by the aggressive armies of the kings of Sweden, while Turkish power continually threatened Poland from the south and bloody Cossack rebellions plagued her in the east. The period of strife with the Teutonic Knights, the Swedes, Cossacks and Turks has been vividly fixed in the memory of the Poles because the famous Polish writer Henryk Sienkiewicz—winner of the Nobel Prize, whose works have been translated into nearly all the languages of the world—described these periods in his historical novels, which are constantly reprinted in hundreds of thousands of copies, and adapted as movies, not only in Poland, but also in the United States, Italy and France.

In the eighteenth century, at the time when the balance of power in Europe was established, the extensive Polish Republic, torn by internal conflicts, found herself surrounded by the three most powerful kingdoms of the time: the empire of Russia, the empire of Austria and the kingdom of Prussia. Each of these powers exerted a constant military and political pressure on their weaker neighbor, in order to subject it entirely to their influences. Poland began to be ruled by foreign ambassadors, who took advantage of the help of the squabbling Polish magnates at odds with the leading state authority as represented by a feeble king. This ended with a political catastrophe without precedence in the history of the world. Toward the end of the eighteenth century, the three adjacent powers came to an agreement with one another, as a result of which the Polish state underwent total liquidation, and the various parts of her territories were incorporated into the partitioning states. This occurred in three successive phases, yet the badly organized and incompetently led Polish Army tried in vain to oppose the armies invading from three directions. Shortly before the last partition a national insurrection broke out against the invaders, led by General Tadeusz Kosciuszko, a hero of the American struggle for independence. Kosciuszko's soldiers, consisting for the most part of hurriedly trained volunteers and peasants armed with scythes, could not win in a battle with the best regular armies of Europe. After some months of desperate struggle, the insurrectionist army was defeated. Kosciuszko, badly wounded, was taken prisoner along with the other leaders. Stanislas Poniatowski, the last king of Poland, was forced to abdicate and deported to St. Petersburg where he died a few years later. The entire country was occupied by hostile powers. The Polish Republic ceased to exist for 120 years. The name of Poland was entirely erased from all the maps of Europe.

During the extended period of enslavement, the Polish people rose several times in desperate insurrections against the partitioning powers. Merciless retaliation followed each of these insurrections. Towns and villages were destroyed, the most precious treasures of Polish culture were looted, police repression intensified. Thousands of the best, most courageous and noble Poles were exiled into the snows of Siberia, or locked up for many years in the prison cells of Prussia and Austrian fortresses.

When the First World War broke out in 1914, the Poles found themselves in a tragic situation. As the subjects of three emperors (the king of Prussia had become the emperor of Germany), they were forced to take part in the war on both sides. Often a Pole, forced into the uniform of a Russian soldier, would unknowingly kill another Pole, wearing a German or Austrian uniform.

As a result of the war and the Russian Revolution, Poland gained independence. But only for twenty years (the Polish state that existed between the two world wars is now called the Second Republic by historians). Then the Second World War began, bringing to our country material and biological destruction on a scale unknown to history.

So this was the background. In periods where all other countries of Europe consistently strengthened the extent of their states and increased the well-being of their populations, catastrophes of war in Poland every decade destroyed the entire

War memorial at Oswiecim

social affluence and everything had to be started from the beginning again.

Surely wars have not left so many scars behind them in any other country as in Poland. All along Polish highways, old Swedish trenches are to be seen alongside Nazi bunkers, the ruins of the castles of Teutonic Knights alongside the graves of nineteenth-century insurrectionists, trenches dating from the First and Second World Wars, moss-grown gravestones of soldiers inscribed in various languages. In every Polish town, the tourist can easily find out how many times in the course of time the town was destroyed, burned down and rebuilt. Near to every other Polish village is some old battlefield, where local collectors dig up from time to time fragments of old Tartar, Swedish or German arms, metal buckles from soldiers' belts with the inscription *Gott mit uns*, and coins with the two-headed eagle of Russian tsars. The littlest village toddler knows that these things once belonged to foreign soldiers who came there to conquer Poland and wreck the lives of her inhabitants.

This is why all Poles develop a hatred of aggressive wars from their childhood days.

THE UNDEFEATED CITY

Warsaw, the capital of the Polish People's Republic, lies halfway along the course of the Vistula (Poland's longest river) and has around 1,250,000 inhabitants.

Warsaw's symbol is the siren, the half-maiden, half-fish of mythology, but differing from other legendary sirens in that she is armed. The origins of this symbol and the circumstances surrounding the origins of the city are lost in the darkness of time, and there is no historical evidence on this topic. Only a legend speaks. According to it, a very long time ago, a couple of poor fishermen lived on the bank of the Vistula, named Wars and Sawa. They were good, hardworking and hospitable people. Thanks to this they gained the favor of one of the sirens who lived in the Vistula at that time. One day the water goddess sent to them a prince of the Vistula territories, who had gone astray in the wilderness. Pleased by the hospitality and other virtues of the poor fishermen, the prince gave them a generous grant of land and allowed them to build a settlement on it, which was later called after its owners as Warsaw.

This legend was assuredly invented by some old teller of tales, but it is very popular among the people of Warsaw. Two large movie houses in Warsaw today are named Wars and Sawa, while the first small-size automobiles manufactured in Poland were christened Sirens. In one of the most picturesque

The river Vistula

parts of the city—the Kosciuszko quay—stands a memorial to the Warsaw siren—a pretty young girl with a fish's tail, armed with sword and shield. This memorial, beloved by the people of Warsaw, survived almost untouched by some miracle from the catastrophes of the last war. However, the young girl who posed for it before the war died the death of a soldier in the memorable days of the Warsaw Insurrection (1944).

Warsaw has been the capital of Poland for only 350 years. In comparison with the thousand-year history of Poland, this is not a very long time. Earlier, for four centuries, the capital was located in Cracow, and still earlier it was in Poznan and Gniezno. The relatively short history of Warsaw as the capital has been filled with stormy and remarkable events. For more than a third of the period, the city was occupied by foreign troops. Here, armed insurrections and street fighting broke out more often than in other cities. The monuments and historical buildings of Warsaw introduce us to such strange and complex matters that foreign tourists are not always able to understand them.

Present-day Warsaw is a lively city being rebuilt and developed at a very brisk tempo. Life in Warsaw is difficult, hurried and nervy. Warsaw generally pleases foreigners. Once they get to know the city, they long remember its special kind of charm, the beauty and charm of the Warsaw girls, the indefatigable vitality and original humor of the city's inhabitants.

The people of Warsaw love their city above all things. Nevertheless, they criticize it constantly and ruthlessly from many aspects. But they lose their tempers when anyone from outside starts to criticize Warsaw. Hearing any such criticism, they grow rigid. Outwardly they politely agree, but inside they think to themselves: "My dear visitor, from far away, what do you really know or understand about it. If you'd been here thirty years ago and during the subsequent years, you'd look differently at everything." For all the people of Warsaw have deeply and painfully engraved in their memories that feature of Warsaw which makes it different from all the other capitals of the world. They know that for a certain time their native city simply did not exist—and that properly speaking it has existed for only twenty-five years.

Introducing Warsaw for the first time to people who do not know the city at all, one should not begin by showing them its superbly rebuilt historical buildings of the seventeenth and eighteenth centuries, or by praising the beauty of the newly built sectors. First of all, one should go back with one's guests to the cruel times of the Nazi occupation. One must unfold before their eyes the sufferings, death and resurrection of the capital with its million inhabitants.

Warsaw siren

The market in the Old City. Warsaw

Every other day, in the evening, Warsaw TV broadcasts a program for children of a puppet serial called "Jacek and Agatha." The family of the two comical puppets talk in funny, childish voices about various contemporary matters of interest to young viewers. They do this so convincingly that the young audience sometimes forgets that Jacek and Agatha are only puppets, not real children. But toward the end of the program the illusion fades. A pleasantly smiling woman appears on the TV screen. And it turns out that it was she who gave her voice to the puppet family.

Few people know the circumstances under which the voices of Jacek and Agatha were heard for the first time. It occurred during the worst period of the Nazi occupation. The woman gifted with the ability to imitate children's voices was working at the time in the resistance movement. On that day several members of the movement, hunted by the Nazis, had gathered at her place. In addition, there were many "compromising" things in the house.

Suddenly the terrifying shriek of an automobile siren was heard in the street—a sound well-known to all inhabitants of Warsaw at that time. Someone glanced out of the window and saw a Gestapo (Nazi secret police) "buda" (paddy wagon) van stop in front of the house. Everyone froze with terror. A visit from the Gestapo in a situation like this must bring with it foreseeable results: the arrest of all present, long interrogations with the most savage torture in order to force out the names of other members of the organization and, in the end, either death or humiliation. When the doorbell rang, the hostess went on tiptoe to the door. And it was precisely then that the voices of Jacek and Agatha were heard. Their worried little voices informed the Gestapo standing outside that they could not open the door because they were by themselves in the apartment and their parents had taken the key when they left, and would not be back until evening. The Gestapo were deluded just like today's viewers. Not wanting, most likely, to scare away the conspirators by a useless search of an empty apartment, they left without a word. It is easy to guess that the apartment was thoroughly cleared of all compromising evidence and the cells of the organization were warned that such-and-such an address was "burned out" (as they said in those days) and must be avoided. In this way Jacek and Agatha—long before their appearance on the TV screen—made a considerable contribution to the underground movement of resistance against the occupiers, bringing about the salvation of several Warsaw patriots.

Such incidents, when echoes of the war and the occupation attack the people of Warsaw at the most unexpected moments, could be multiplied. But is it necessary to refer to incidents? After all, the horrors of those inhuman times are constantly brought to mind by the walls of rebuilt Warsaw houses and the memorials of Warsaw—which the inhabitants of the capital pass by almost every day, both when they are hurrying to daily work in factories and offices, and when they enjoy holiday strolls around the city.

You tourist from far away taking your first stroll around Warsaw, keep an eye open and look attentively at the walls of buildings which you pass. Do this most of all in the most frequented main streets of the capital: in noisy, crowded Marszalkowska Street; in Ujazdowski Boulevard romantically shaded by trees; in capriciously curved New World Street, to which postwar architects have returned its eighteenth-century beauty; in broad and dignified Cracow Boulevard, filled with old churches and historic palaces. In each of these streets can be found inscriptions engraved on the walls of houses, before which passersby raise their hats and schoolchildren every now and then place a wreath of flowers and light mourning candles.

You visitor from far away, read these inscriptions on the

walls of Warsaw with attention. They mark the places made sacred by the blood of Poles, shed during the occupation for the freedom of their country and city. In front of this house, for instance, the Nazis shot two hundred hostages—two hundred peaceable civilians, driven from their houses at night. In front of that house, a long line of men and women stood faced by the rifles of uniformed murderers, with their lips plastered so that they could not cry out even when dying. Several hundred young Scouts were murdered by this wall, caught putting up patriotic pamphlets. This memorial stone marks the place where soldiers of the Polish underground army carried out just revenge for all these crimes on one of the bloodiest Nazi executioners—Frank Kutsche, commander of the SS and police of the Warsaw district, who organized mass murders not only in Poland, but also in Czechoslovakia, Denmark, Holland, Yugoslavia and the U.S.S.R.

There is an uncountable number of such memorials in Warsaw. They are to be found in all parts of the city. The walls of Warsaw shout aloud, they accuse and will not let us forget. Even though for some unknown reason Warsaw wanted to free itself from the nightmare of the past, the city must always remember that it is the capital of a country which lost six million citizens in the last war, i.e., a fifth of its population, more than any other country in the world.

The monuments of Warsaw also remind us of this. Here is one of the representative squares—Theater Square. Two of the oldest theaters of the capital are located here: the National Theater and the Grand Theater. Totally destroyed during the war, they have been rebuilt still more splendid than before. During the last decade, several productions at the National Theater have won a European reputation. The Grand Theater is the largest opera stage in Europe.

A few years ago, Theater Square acquired a new architectural feature—the Heroes of Warsaw monument. On a high, massive plinth a girl of stone with flowing hair and inspired face raises a sword over her head, about to strike, while her other hand is raised in a gesture either of victory or despair— no one knows. She floats thus in the air. The creators of the monument succeeded in giving precisely this impression— floating in the air.

This monument, which won the hearts of the people of Warsaw from the first and has become the destination of all tourist pilgrimages—is generally known as the Nike of Warsaw. And in fact it is reminiscent of the statue of the Greek goddess of victory. But it is also reminiscent in some way of the monument on the Vistula bank of the Warsaw siren. It is a new Warsaw siren—stirred from her motionless peace, brought to life by just anger and the desire to fight. It symbolizes the Warsaw of the war and occupation years—overthrown, but still fighting. Who knows but maybe that young girl who posed for the monument on the Kosciuszko quay looked just so before her death.

On days of solemn anniversaries associated with those years, artistic displays are held at the Warsaw Heroes monument. They are unusual and impressive. The great square is flooded by countless crowds of people. Only the monument is lit up. The girl of stone, with a sword in her hand, rises in the bright white light of searchlights above the still and silent crowd. Melodious words, interspersed with music, resound from the foot of the monument. The most celebrated artists of Warsaw recite the poems of twenty-year-old poets who died fighting for the freedom of the capital. Sometimes poetry gives way to prose. Those reciting, lowering resounding voices and giving them the most ordinary sound, utter the text of speeches which have nothing to do with literature but speak of everyday matters of the besieged city: difficulties with supplies, erecting defensive earthworks and barricades, how to act during air raids. But from time to time, the words "Warsaw defends itself and will

The Nikè monument. Warsaw

On the monument base:

BOHATEROM
WARSZAWY
1939-1945

defend itself!" resound more loudly from the monotonous text with its practical advice and instructions.

A powerful shudder of emotion runs through the crowds silently flooding Theater Square. Half of the listeners remember these words from those years when they were uttered over the radio by Stefan Starzynski, the civilian Commissioner of Defense for Warsaw.

Starzynski was the prewar mayor of the capital. Many Warsaw people knew him by sight from the times when he liked to sit alone on summer afternoons on the open terrace of the Europe Cafe, where today too many highly placed individuals are often to be seen. He was short, heavily built, with an ordinary face, and nothing in his appearance indicated a hero. Yet later—in September 1939—he showed he was a hero.

Some days after the outbreak of war, when the president, the government, the high command and most of the central authorities were evacuating the bombed capital so as soon to be beyond the frontiers of Poland—Stefan Starzynski took over the "government of souls" in Warsaw. Not the generals commanding the military garrison of the city, but he, an ordinary, unpretentious civilian, became the brain and heart of the heroic defense of the city. For three terrible weeks of siege, when fires raged in the city, houses collapsed under ceaseless bombing, when there was no water, gas or electricity, when food and ammunition were running out, Starzynski spoke on the radio every evening to the population. With the hoarse, worn voice of a deadly tired man, sometimes assuredly hungry too, he encouraged the people of Warsaw and urged them on to continue defense. He did not promise victory, as victory was impossible. All he wanted was for the world to notice the desperate struggle of Warsaw, to regard that struggle as an example for itself. And Warsaw defended itself fiercely. It defended itself as long as an open city can, crushed on all sides by iron and fire. His aim was gained. Not long after the surrender of the city, the Prime Minister of the powerful British Empire, Winston Churchill, in a historic speech broadcast by the radio stations of all free nations, called Warsaw "an inspiration for the world."

When the Nazi armies entered Warsaw, Starzynski was arrested. For several days he was subjected to the most terrible torture, then shot. But his heroism—gray and not effective, so different from the colorful and dramatic heroism demonstrated in the favorite historical readings of Poles—did not pass without an echo. Thousands of fervent imitators were found among the soldiers and activists of the Warsaw underground movement.

"The Warsaw underground! . . . underground Warsaw! . . . underground Poland!" Every Pole knows what these phrases meant. But the idea must be explained to readers who know the history of the occupation in Poland only through indirect and general reports.

From almost the first day of the German occupation, Warsaw began living a double life. On one side it was the *Stadt Warschau,* the occupied, administrative center created by the Germans and called the "General Government," a city in which the stern laws of merciless victors ruled. In this city only elementary schools existed for Poles, since higher education "for people of a lesser race" was not necessary. The Poles were not allowed to leave their homes in the evenings, because curfew was observed from 7 P.M., and a delayed pedestrian risked death. Jews and Poles of Jewish origin were thrown out of their homes and crowded behind the walls of the ghetto. The entire Polish population was expelled from the best parts of the city, which were seized for use by Germans. Notices saying "Germans Only" were placed on many restaurants, stores and streetcars, and Poles were not allowed to enter them. The German political police rounded up by night the most respected citizens and deported them from their homes to concentration camps. People were seized at the most unexpected times of day in the most crowded streets. Hundreds of chance passersby were loaded into trucks and sent to labor camps during these "roundups," as they were known in occupation slang. The city lived in an atmosphere of constant terror. Whenever an automobile stopped at night outside a house, it caused alarm; whenever the doorbell rang, it made people's hearts beat faster.

But in addition to the Warsaw dominated and ruled by the occupiers there existed another Warsaw—illegal, evading the authority of the invaders. It was a city which "had gone underground" (no one knows who first used this poetical metaphor).

Underground Warsaw did not capitulate to Hitler's power and maintained independence. It continued to be the capital of fighting Poland—the main center of the whole country's resistance movement.

Underground Warsaw did not recognize the regulations of the occupying authorities. It countered them in an active, constructive way. Everything the Nazis destroyed and annihilated in the captured city was rebuilt in its underground. The occupiers closed high schools, but in hundreds of private homes, guarded by sentries, patriotic teachers and professors belonging to the resistance movement did secret teaching, of which tens of thousands of young people of Warsaw took advantage. The Germans held officers and soldiers taken prisoner after the collapse of the 1939 campaign in concentration camps—but more soldiers and officers were trained in the Warsaw underground. Underground Warsaw had its commanding officers who directed the resistance movement across the entire country. It also had its own lawcourts which passed sentence in the name of the Polish Republic on Nazi hangmen and traitors collaborating with the occupiers. Patriotic newspapers and leaflets were printed in secret printing presses, which youthful distributors circulated around the whole city, at the risk of their own lives. Emissaries of the Warsaw underground penetrated into the walls of the ghetto, providing food and arms to a resistance movement unit there. A special section worked on manufacturing forged ID papers for "burned out" members of the conspiracy and for Jews hiding outside the ghetto. Patriotic cultural life developed in underground Warsaw. In hidden private places, literary and musical evenings were held, and even theatrical productions. It was here that poets and writers who today occupy the leading positions in Polish literature first read their poems and stories, as did those who later died as soldiers in the Insurrection, or who were murdered in concentration camps.

The Nazi occupiers feared underground Warsaw. For each of their acts of terror brought about an immediate response from the underground. In revenge for street executions, for the torturing of prisoners in the Gestapo jails, for the deporting of thousands of innocent people to the concentration camps—soldiers of the resistance movement carried out attacks on Nazi dignitaries, threw bombs into places where Nazi officers gathered, blew up military railroad transports, committed innumerable acts of sabotage which disorganized German war industry.

As Nazi terror intensified, so the resistance movement gained in strength, until the time finally came when underground Warsaw emerged from hiding and stood up to open battle with the occupiers. On August 1, 1944, at 5 P.M., units of young soldiers with red and white armbands emerged from the gates of Warsaw houses and national flags flew over the occupied city Armed Insurrection had broken out in the capital of Poland.

Many books on the Warsaw Insurrection have appeared in Poland during the past decade. Historians and former Insurrectionists have made a detailed analysis of the Insurrection operation from the point of view of strategy and politics. Many reproaches have been made in these books about the emigree Polish government which issued the call to arms from London without assuring appropriate help and without fully thinking out its chances and results in the over-all military and political situation of that time. Inadequate military preparation for the Insurrection and lack of co-operation between Insurrection high command and the high command of the approaching Soviet offensive have been criticized. But none of these critical comments can or attempt to diminish the magnificent impulse of the people of the city, who, after five years of terrible and destructive occupation, threw off the yoke of enslavement by their own powers and fought for two months with unparalleled courage and devotion against an enemy many times stronger, awakening the admiration of the whole world and writing one of the most heroic and dramatic pages in the history of World War II.

In the blaze of searchlights illuminating the monument in Theater Square all those whom Warsaw honors as its heroes are brought back to life: Mayor Starzynski and the defenders of the capital in September 1939; activists of the underground put to death in the cells of the Gestapo because they refused to betray their comrades in the struggle; patriotic teachers and journalists who paid with their lives for secretly teaching young people and publishing underground newspapers; youthful fighters of the resistance movement who took revenge on the hangmen of Warsaw for their inhuman crimes; citizens of the capital shot for helping their Jewish fellow citizens; heroic soldiers of the Warsaw Insurrection who gave back independence for two months to the occupied city; fifteen-year-old distributors of newspapers and Boy Scouts who—armed only with bottles of gasoline—hurled themselves at German tanks belching fire; beautiful Warsaw girls who ruled during the last prewar carnival at student dances and who, during the Insurrection, dirty and in rags, crept under a hail of bullets, carrying wounded soldiers; ten-year-old Insurrectionist messenger boys who, sneaking with reports from one sector of the city to another, had to hold seized German helmets from slipping down over their eyes, and who were scolded by their mothers on returning from these dangerous trips; and the thousands of ordinary Warsaw citizens who perished just for being Poles!

The crowds at the monument of the Heroes of Warsaw, remembering them all, recall at the same time their own nearest and dearest. For there is certainly not one family in Warsaw which did not suffer one painful loss during the occupation. Suffice it to say that during the Insurrection alone, about 200,000 people of Warsaw were killed or murdered.

A special monument honors the memory of the victims and heroes of the Warsaw ghetto. It is located in the northern sector of the city, on the former area of the closed Jewish sector which the occupiers created. Today one of the largest residential areas of the city, Muranow, is located here. The busiest main streets of the city run by the square with the monument to the Heroes of the Ghetto. Around the square, in the windows of the buildings on the large, modern residential blocks are neat curtains. Children play happily in the little gardens in front of the houses. It is difficult, not only for foreign tourists but also for most of the present-day inhabitants of Warsaw, to imagine that less than thirty years ago one of the most terrible hells, invented by the Nazis, was located here, shut off by walls from the rest of the city. But the monument bears witness.

A simple granite wall symbolizes the walls of the ghetto, while two bronze reliefs provide an impressive survey of its history. One shows a group of Jews being driven to execution, the other a unit of fighters of the resistance movement who took part in the desperate Insurrection inside the ghetto. The

Ghetto monument. Warsaw

monument is the work of a Jewish sculptor and a Polish architect. It was constructed in granite which the Germans brought to Warsaw, toward the end of the occupation, as material for a monument to Hitler.

The Warsaw ghetto was one of the main stages of the campaign for the total annihilation of the Jews. The occupiers shut up in it 500,000 Polish citizens from Warsaw and other cities who were regarded as Jews on the basis of the Nazi "race laws." Inside the ghetto, believers in the Mosaic religion and Christians of various denominations found themselves side by side with people who felt Jewish and people with many generations of Polish blood. Among the last-named were many famous Polish scholars and artists.

The enormous crowding of houses, starvation-level rations of food, lack of medicine and fuel, separation from society annihilated the population of the ghetto. Now and then the Nazis carried out what were called "liquidation campaigns." Many thousands of the population of the ghetto were deported to camps of mass annihilation at Treblinka, where they were massacred in gas chambers and burned to ash in crematoriums.

In April 1943 the occupiers decided to carry out the final liquidation of the ghetto, in which only 70,000 inhabitants remained. But this time they encountered unexpected resistance. The underground Jewish Fighting Organization, which had been in contact with the Warsaw resistance movement for a long time, now declared war against the Germans.

On April 23, 1943, the *Voice of Warsaw*, a secret newspaper of the Polish Workers' Party, reported:

> On Sunday at 2 A.M., Nazi bands treacherously attacked the Warsaw ghetto. A bloodthirsty orgy began. Hangmen of the SS dragged women and children out of their homes. Children's heads were smashed on the sidewalks. The population was driven into the square in order to force them along the notorious route to the gas chambers of Treblinka. But this time the Nazi murderers miscalculated . . . The Warsaw ghetto has been preparing for many months to defend itself. The Nazis' attempts to isolate the Jews entirely from the rest of the world failed. The slogan "For our and your freedom" found clear expression in the assistance given by the Polish population in preparing self-defense in the ghetto. The massacre was calculated for a brief deadline. It has been transformed into a stubborn battle which has already lasted many days . . . It is difficult to speak of the heroic efforts of the Jewish population without deep admiration and respect . . . The red and white banner raised on the

church tower in the ghetto has grown to a symbol . . . As a result of the unexpected attack there are Poles in the ghetto now fighting shoulder to shoulder with Jews in the ghetto streets against Germans. A feeling of solidarity with the fighting Jews continually intensifies . . .

After the repression of the Insurrection, the Nazis razed the Warsaw ghetto. For a long time, the echoes of explosions were to be heard in Warsaw. Underground bunkers in which Insurrectionists had taken refuge were being blown up with dynamite. About 20,000 people died in the battle or were burned alive. The Nazis murdered the remainder of the population in the gas chambers of Treblinka. Thanks to the help of Polish underground organizations, several groups of Insurrectionists were brought out of the ghetto and enabled to continue partisan fighting.

When paying tribute to the heroes of the Warsaw ghetto, Dr. Janusz Korczak must be mentioned. This great educator and humanist who enriched Polish literature with his fine books about children and who gained enormous popularity in prewar Warsaw with his radio series "Talks of an Old Doctor" devoted the last decade of his life to educating poor Jewish orphans. On the day war broke out, Korczak (who was a lieutenant colonel of the Polish Army Reserve) put on his officer's uniform. Some months later he made his way in this uniform along with his orphans to the ghetto. In August 1942, during the first large-scale liquidation campaign, the Jewish orphanage was deported to Treblinka. Apparently it was wished to save Korczak from death, but he refused. The few witnesses who succeeded in surviving the ghetto have always remembered the impressive picture of the Old Doctor's last journey. A long column of children surrounded by a cordon of howling gendarmes. At its head, holding the smallest child by the hand, the short, bald man with a beard, wearing a shabby officer's uniform and the star of David on his sleeve. Apparently, Korczak told the children fairy tales all the way to death. He told them on the way to the railroad station in the ghetto. Later, he told them in the cattle car which was so packed that people died standing up. And even later, in Treblinka, as they were entering the gas chambers . . .

It is not easy to pass from the nightmare recollections associated with the monument to the Heroes of the Ghetto to two other Warsaw monuments which are also associated with the occupation, but in an entirely different manner. Anecdotes connected with them testify that a sense of humor did not desert the people of Warsaw even during the hardest times—and that it also played a certain role in the fight against the occupiers.

In Warsaw's Old City—conjured up by a miracle after the war from ruins and ashes—stands a monument to the popular hero of this district, Jan Kilinski. This Old City tailor, named colonel by Kosciuszko for the courage he showed, is represented by the creator of his monument in an unusually military attitude. This is assuredly how Kilinski looked on April 17, 1794, when at the head of the people of Warsaw he drove the army of Catherine the Great from the city. The Nazi occupiers found it hard to tolerate this monument which clearly called for armed resistance against foreign domination. This was why the bronze figure was removed from its plinth in the winter of 1943 and placed in the cellars of the National Museum. But the lads of the Warsaw underground did not leave this act without a reply. By the next day, the entire façade of the National Museum was painted with a huge inscription: "People of Warsaw, I am here—Kilinski." This was not all: another notice appeared on the monument of the great Polish astronomer Copernicus, which stands in Cracow Boulevard: "As punishment for the removal of Kilinski, I lengthen the winter by two months. Copernicus." And we should bear in mind that this was the winter of Stalingrad, so terrible for the Germans, and a joke like this must have irritated them considerably.

Another anecdote of the occupation is associated with the column of King Zygmunt in Castle Square. This monument, erected in the seventeenth century, is the capital's oldest and most beautiful symbol. It is a favorite topic for poets and a favorite resting place for birds flying across Warsaw. On a 50-foot-high slender column stands the statue of King Zygmunt III of the Vasa family. This king does not have a good reputation in Polish history. He engaged the country in various unnecessary wars, let the Jesuits lead him by the nose and was marked by a lack of tolerance rare in the rulers of Poland. But the people of Warsaw forgive him all this because it was he who transferred the capital of the state from Cracow to Warsaw. This is also why he has been given such a high position.

Shortly before the outbreak of the Warsaw Insurrection, a German convoy taking money from the bank note factory was attacked in broad daylight close to the Zygmunt column. The loot acquired by the attackers amounted to 120 million zlotys and 25 million German marks, while several Nazi gendarmes were killed in the incident. A week afterward, posters appeared in the city announcing an award of 5 million zlotys for anyone who could indicate those responsible for the attack. Next day, the following letter came to the German police:

> I hereby apply as ready to provide the most detailed information about the entire incident, of which I was the nearest witness. Standing on my column, I saw everything from beginning to end. I decline the award on behalf of the poor of the city of Warsaw. I make one condition: I will provide the information when, without using a ladder, you kiss my a—.
>
> Zygmunt III, *King.*

Statue of Copernicus. Warsaw

Castle Square and the monument of King Zygmunt III. Warsaw

You must forgive His Majesty the King his rather vulgar joke. At that time, everyone in Warsaw was a soldier, and no one was particularly careful in his choice of words. In any case, Zygmunt III's good humor did not last long. A few months later, after the collapse of the Insurrection, the witty monarch underwent the sad fate of all Warsaw monuments.

Enraged by the "rebellion" of Warsaw, Hitler ordered its total annihilation. The sentence was carried out with horrifying accuracy. The entire population of the left bank of Warsaw (the district of Praga, on the right bank of the Vistula, was liberated in mid-September 1944 by the Soviet offensive) was evacuated to a transit camp near Pruszkow. Those who did not manage in some way to get out were then deported either to concentration camps or to forced-labor camps. Special units of the SS, armed with flamethrowers, entered the deserted city with fire bombs and other destructive weapons. House after house, monument after monument were burned and destroyed. Soon the city of a million people was changed into a huge cemetery of ruins. The cultural inheritance gathered by tens of generations through several centuries was lost. Among others, the tall monument of Zygmunt III was destroyed. The column, hymned by poets, was overturned, and the first Warsaw king fell face downward to the street of his own capital. The city of Wars and Sawa ceased to exist.

Soldiers of the First Polish Army, fighting shoulder to shoulder with the Soviet Army, watched the death of Warsaw from the Praga bank with tears in their eyes and despair in their hearts. The core of this reborn Polish Army was the division named after Tadeusz Kosciuszko formed in 1943 in the Soviet Union from Poles who, as a result of the war, found themselves in Soviet territory. The general plan of the great offensive, which had not taken into account the outbreak of the Insurrection, made it impossible for Polish soldiers to come to the effective aid of the Insurrectionists. During the last phase of the Insurrection, the First Polish Army lost some four thousand soldiers and officers during the crossing of the Vistula and in fighting on the bridgeheads.

On January 17, 1945, as a result of the new Soviet-Polish offensive, the massacred remains of Warsaw were torn from the

Nazis. Polish soldiers were greeted by a landscape of eerie terror: the projecting foundations of smashed bridges, dead streets strewn with mountains of rubble, the burned-out skeletons of houses, palaces and churches, overturned streetcars, monuments hurled from their plinths, a deathly emptiness and silence, not disturbed by any echo of life. This city was not destroyed—it had been crushed in the mortar of war.

The former inhabitants of Warsaw began arriving in crowds at the burned-out site immediately after the army. They came from all directions: from Praga, from nearby villages, from other cities, from liberated Nazi concentration camps. In those days the same thing could be seen on all roads around Warsaw: tanks, artillery and infantry of the great offensive moving west, while innumerable columns of loaded carts and pedestrians weighed down by bags or handcarts passed along the side in the direction of Warsaw. These were the evacuated people of Warsaw returning to their homes, although these homes no longer existed.

The new leadership of the reborn state, which appeared in Lublin after the liberation of the first Polish territories, at first considered whether a city as destroyed as Warsaw could carry out the function of the main political and administrative center of the country, and whether it would not be better to transfer the capital during the first period of rebuilding to undamaged Lodz (a great center of the textile industry and the second largest city in Poland). However, a more difficult decision was reached which corresponded not only to the wishes of the people of Warsaw but also to those of the entire nation: the capital must remain in Warsaw, as that would bring about the more rapid reconstruction of the heroic city. Only a few days after the armies had entered the city, the political and administrative authorities of the Third Republic began governing in crowded apartments of ugly apartment

Warsaw in 1945

houses of undamaged Praga. The city, slain by the Nazis, awakened to a new life as the capital of People's Poland.

This process of resurrection was accomplished in indescribably hard and complicated conditions. Poland was not yet entirely liberated. Fierce fighting was still going on on all fronts of the world war. The frontiers and regime of the new Polish state were the subject of discussion at international conferences. In addition to the provisional Polish government, consisting of leaders of the left-wing underground and democratic political activists who had spent the war in the Soviet Union, there was also the former emigree government in London, recognized by the Western powers and firmly opposed to the political and social changes occurring in Poland. Many former soldiers of the underground took to the forests with their arms, to await further instructions from London. Meanwhile in Poland the II Corps of the Polish Army was urgently formed, and was to take part with the I Corps in the decisive Soviet offensive against the final defensive positions of the Nazis. Simultaneously radical economic reforms were hastily realized. People who had not yet been able to take off their army uniforms or wadded partisan jackets now divided the lands of prewar landowners to landless or small holding peasants and took over control of large private industries in the name of the people. Almost every day trucks left Praga for the west with "operational groups" of officials and militia to organize the Polish administration in the territories on the Oder, Nysa and Baltic liberated by the Soviet offensive. After centuries of German rule, these territories were to return once again to Poland.

It was in this international and internal situation, in an atmosphere intoxicated with freedom and painful political dissension, accompanied by joyful greeting of the living and mourning for the dead, that the rebuilding of the Polish capital began.

The constant influx of people meant that soon the dead ruins of the city took on the appearance of some enormous nomad camp. The returning people of Warsaw were forced by necessity to become modern Robinson Crusoes (one of the first movies produced in Poland after the war was entitled *Warsaw Robinson*). They had to acquire everything necessary for life with their own hands and inventiveness. In the unheated ruins of houses, holes in the walls and ceilings were patched with planks, blankets replaced windowpanes and the "rebuilt" apartments were furnished with scraps of furniture dug out from the ruins. Getting into these apartments, especially when they were on upper floors, often required acrobatic talent and meant risking one's life, or injury. Inventive Warsaw traders organized the first "bars" in wrecked streetcars, serving hot dinners. Former representative squares of the capital came to resemble small-town marketplaces. Peasants from the surrounding villages traveled to them with carts filled with various country products. But as the old money had already lost its value and the new currency was not trusted, trade was mostly by exchange. Butter was exchanged for clothes, linen for cheese, chairs for tables, tables for chairs, tea for cigarettes, cigarettes for tea, etc. The first "coupons" for workers' canteens and the first "ration cards" for certain goods in the state stores in Praga appeared. The only link with Praga was a wooden pontoon bridge, but people also crossed on the ice, which did not always end happily. Peasants' carts and ancient trucks covered with tarpaulins stood in the busiest parts of the city. Their owners loudly praised their services, and hoarse cries of "To Praga! To Praga!"—with the characteristic Vistula accent—resounded in the ears of the weary people of Warsaw like an invitation to the most luxurious automobile.

In the city once famed for the proverbial Warsaw chic, the favorite costume of men became shabby army coats without shoulder straps and greasy berets, and the favorite attire of women was ordinary woolen scarves. People were not ashamed of being poor; on the contrary: it was flourished before the eyes of newcomers from other, undestroyed cities. Proud poverty became the new Warsaw chic. In the capital stripped of all its charms, it was not the thing to be well dressed, to live and eat well.

In this first period of the "great Robinsonade," an article of special value much sought after was ordinary chalk. It replaced the mail for families divided by the war and the outbreak of the Insurrection. On the walls of wrecked Warsaw houses—alongside tar inscriptions *MIN NET* (No mines) left by Soviet sappers—appeared information intimate or public by nature drawn in chalk. Here is a litany written down by a chronicler of those days from the walls of a house: "Zocha, I am looking for you everywhere! I'll be here Tuesday at noon. Your Gieniek." . . . "Dear family! We are staying with Aunt Hela in Praga. Witek, Basia and the children." . . . "I am looking for the Kwiatkowski family from the second floor. Anyone with news, please let the Zalewskis in the basement know." . . . "Death to the Bolshevik stooges!" . . . "Let's wring the neck of the hydra of reaction!" . . . "The stupid painter lost the war." . . . "Uncle Anselm Golkowski died in the Old City. Olek. I am in army unit no. . . ."

Every day mass clearing of streets and squares took place. Everyone took part in this campaign. Shovel in hand, Communist Party officials and ministers, scholars and artists, students and schoolchildren, women and children, workers and soldiers worked side by side. They worked with genuine enthusiasm and in an excellent mood. Every square yard of surface cleared foreshadowed a new street, every whole brick saved from the ruins was the down payment for a new house.

But in the evenings and at night Warsaw became terrible. You could walk for miles through an icy, gloomy wilderness spiked with the stalagmites of ruins, not illuminated by a single light. Even worse was the fact that this wilderness had its own deceptive mirages. Around the corner suddenly there might appear a cheerful red streetcar. But joyful surprise rapidly passed, for it was not a "live" streetcar, but a corpse. It is hard to describe how desperately people longed for the ordinary, normal life of a great city.

But time passed and brought more and more changes. The Soviet and Polish armies took Berlin. The Nazi Third Reich, planned to last a thousand years, capitulated to the victors after a decade of existence filled with monstrous crimes against humanity. Poland's new frontiers were laid down at an international conference. The provisional government became the

Government of National Unity. Emigree politicians from London entered it. A referendum and general elections confirmed the new regime. In the temporary offices of the Warsaw Ministry of Foreign Affairs, diplomatic staffs were urgently recruited for appointments in foreign capitals which officially recognized People's Poland in large numbers. Throughout the country communications were rebuilt, factories started production and the structure of the countryside was altered. The western territories, deserted by the Germans, were settled. Tens of thousands of illiterate people were taught to read and write. More and more new schools and higher institutes of education were opened. Two working-class parties (the Polish Working Party and the Polish Socialist Party) united to form the United Polish Workers' Party. Soldiers, militia and teachers perished in fratricidal battles with opponents of the new regime. Supporters of the new ideology were forced to eat their party ID cards before being shot. Many innocent people were victims of false accusation and unjust sentences. Painful human dramas were played out in the forests. Members of the "forest units" gave themselves up, after varying periods of hesitation, to the authorities, and tried to join in normal life, though this did not always take place without difficulties.

Meanwhile Warsaw had passed from the period of the "great Robinsonade" to the period of "great rebuilding."

The first streetcar line was started as early as 1945. For the people of Warsaw this was an event as unusual and marvelous as Stephenson's first railroad had been, 120 years earlier, for the British. Every day, week and month brought new events: the first entirely rebuilt house . . . the first theater . . . the first movie house . . . the first store with ready-made clothes . . . the first nursery for children . . . the first telephone exchange . . .

On every July Holiday (July 22 marks the anniversary of the publication of the principles of the new regime, and is

Spiral approach road to the Poniatowski Bridge

celebrated in People's Poland as the most important state holiday) some great new investment is put into public use: the Poniatowski Bridge . . . the Mariensztat district . . . the East-West Highway . . . the Marszalkowska residential district . . . the rebuilt industrial factories in Wola . . . the factory of private automobiles in Zeran . . . the Warsaw steel foundry . . .

The slogan "The entire nation is building its own capital" was not a mere phrase. Apart from the huge sums of money donated to Warsaw from the state budget, there was also a Social Fund for the Rebuilding of the Capital, increased by voluntary contributions from the whole of society. Along with the people of Warsaw, Warsaw was rebuilt by miners from Silesia, textile workers from Lodz, port workers from the Baltic and mountaineers from the Tatras.

Warsaw's East Wall. Modern buildings

On Sunday afternoons crowds of the people of Warsaw—mostly with children—assembled to admire or criticize new projects. Surely the people of Warsaw had never felt themselves to be so much the owners of their city. They raised it from nothingness with their own hands and then, taking part in public discussions over the architectural and urbanistic plans, decided its future shape.

In this fervent rebuilding of Warsaw, as sacrificial and heroic as the previous Robinsonade and the wartime underground, were elements which every foreigner must have found very strange.

Imagine, if you can, that a new city is to be built on the burned-out site of a city of which, as is said in Poland, "not one stone remains on another." Any urbanist or architect would recognize that as a dream for creating a completely modern city, completely free of the ballast of the past and suited to the needs of the present day in every particular. But the people directing the rebuilding of the capital of Poland thought somewhat otherwise, as they were people of Warsaw. And all the people of Warsaw fervently wanted their rebuilt capital to be a modern city, but that at the same time it stay the old Warsaw. The people did not and could not agree with the irrevocable loss of the historic little streets of the Old City where, as Juliusz Slowacki the great Polish poet wrote, "Kilinski's green eyes frighten us" and where the bitter fighting of the Warsaw Insurrectionists took place in 1944. The people would have felt themselves strange without their beloved though not always very beautiful monuments, without their old palaces, churches and marketplaces—closely associated with great events of olden times and overgrown with modern history from the years of the last war. This longing for ruined monuments had nothing in common with conservatism. The people of Warsaw have never been conservatives. For centuries they have marched in the avant-garde of Polish progress. It was from them that appeals for national insurrections and social revolutions came. In the period of the great Robinsonade after the war, they also showed they were not marked by any exaggerated attachment to material goods. But they loved the heroic and progressive biography of their city, so they had the right to demand that all evidence of this biography be resurrected from the ashes of the war.

Here we may use as an example the characteristic history of the rebuilding of the Frédéric Chopin monument. The greatest Polish musician and one of the greatest musicians of the world was organically linked with Warsaw. To be sure, he was born in a small manor house outside Warsaw, but he spent half his life in Warsaw. It was here he learned music, here his first fame radiated and here he fell in love for the first time. A certain eminent foreign specialist in Chopin's music recently admitted to journalists that Chopin's music cannot be understood to the depths without a knowledge of Warsaw and its surroundings. And she was surely right. Because in Chopin's music are to be found not only the landscapes and mood of his closest family districts but also echoes of the stormy history of Warsaw. Not in vain did Robert Schumann, the great German composer, call his music "cannons hidden in flowers."

No one knows whether the Nazis knew this opinion of their great countryman. In any case, they adopted a hostile attitude toward Chopin (for playing Chopin's works the death penalty was threatened). As early as 1940 his monument in Lazienki Park was overturned by order of the occupiers, cut into pieces and sent to Germany.

The people of Warsaw before the war did not care for this monument. Many faults were seen in it and many malicious jokes about it were circulated. But when after the war it began to be considered whether a competition for a new Chopin monument project should be held, an uproar of protests immediately arose. The people of Warsaw did not want a new monument, even though it might be a hundred times finer than the destroyed one. They wanted Chopin to be as before, because that monument had undergone a Warsaw occupation death, for many people still remembered the terrible sight of Chopin's severed head being driven in a railroad car into the heart of Germany. And the monument of the great musician was rebuilt in its prewar—so often questioned—shape and it stands as earlier in Lazienki Park. On summer afternoons young pianists perform at its foot, many of whom had not been born before the war.

As Lazienki Park has been mentioned, it is worth devoting a few words to this most beautiful public park in Warsaw and its curious history.

In the second half of the eighteenth century, the extensive Lazienki gardens, with their exquisite palace, theater on the island and many other treasures of the architecture and art of that time, were the favorite summer residence of the last king of Poland, Stanislas Augustus Poniatowski.

The people of Warsaw have an ambiguous attitude toward this monarch: on the one hand they condemn him as causer of the partitions of the state and guilty of the loss of independence, but on the other they remember him gratefully as an enlightened reformer, a patron of learning and art who adorned the capital with many beautiful buildings, leaving on it the impress of his own style, known as "Augustan" from his name.

Stanislas Poniatowski came to the throne in a somewhat peculiar manner. His social origins did not predestine him for this. Contemporary rumor had it (as the king was often offensively reminded later) that his grandfather had been something like the manager or even an ordinary official on the estate of a magnate. But his father—thanks to his military prowess, greatness of character and high intelligence and above all

Monument to Frédéric Chopin. Warsaw

Palace in Lazienki Park

thanks to his marrying a young lady from one of the oldest and most powerful aristocratic families—entered the social hierarchy, attained high state offices and finally stood at the head of the most influential group of magnates in Poland.

Stanislas Augustus inherited unusual intelligence, political skill and enthusiasm for reform from his father, whom he even excelled in education and culture, though he differed from him totally in character. He was a weak individual, hesitant and fond of good living. From his youth he had been sent by his family to foreign diplomatic service and for a long time he resided in St. Petersburg, the capital of the Russian Empire, first as a secretary of the British embassy, later as the Saxon ambassador. There he was initiated into the secrets of great politics, translated Shakespeare into Polish and enjoyed himself. At a ball he met the young wife of the Russian heir to the throne, Catherine, betrayed and ill-treated by her limited husband. A serious love affair started between the two young people, which was to have a decisive influence on Poniatowski's future. Some years later his adored Catherine removed her detested husband and came to the throne of Russia as the autocratic Empress Catherine the Great.

The powerful ruler did not forget her Polish romance. Knowing his weak character and attachment to her, she decided to make use of him as a tool for acquiring decisive influence over the Polish state, which was collapsing internally. After the death of Augustus (August) III, the king of Poland of the Saxon dynasty, she gave her support at the elections to Poniatowski and despite the wishes of most of the gentry, she paved his way to the throne.

The rule of the last king was stormy and it ended in tragedy. It was never forgotten that he had gained the crown with the help of foreign bayonets. Several times attempts were made on his life (the organizer of one was Kazimierz Pulaski, who later fled from the police to the United States where he was famed as a hero of the War of Independence). Despite all his good will and undeniable talents, Stanislas Augustus failed to cure the anarchy of the gentry Republic. His patriotic efforts toward strengthening and modernizing Poland did not agree with the blind obedience demanded by the powerful neighboring ruler, in whom the king still saw his beloved and loving "Sophie" of the days of his St. Petersburg romance.

Stanislas Augustus took refuge in the delightful Lazienki gardens from the cares of great politics. Here, surrounded by poets, scholars, architects and beautiful women, he enjoyed poetry, dreamed plans of reform, confirmed projects of new, progressive laws and beautiful new buildings. Here in solitude he lived through the bitterness of the first partition of the state. Here, weeping with emotion, he heard cheering in the streets in his honor after the passing by the Sejm (Assembly) of the progressive Constitution of May 3, 1791. Here, three years later, during the Kosciuszko insurrection, he received leaflets with anonymous verses starting with the words: "The king betrayed his people, so he is to be killed." Finally, in late fall, after the collapse of the insurrection, he came here for the last time to bid goodbye to his beloved residence before setting out, guarded by the troops of his adored "Sophie," into exile, from which he did not return.

In the shady alleys of Lazienki Park, in front of the white palace reflected so charmingly in the mirror of a lake, the melancholy atmosphere of those faded events can still be felt. And it is hard to resist the thought that Poland really is a very strange country. For had this enlightened and talented Stanislas Augustus ruled in a different, less hopeless historical situation, who knows but that he would have gone down in the memory of Poles as one of their best rulers.

But to return to the peculiarities of the postwar "great rebuilding." It went ahead on two tracks. On the one hand, a new, modern city was being built. No prewar models cramped the style. Remains of old buildings were blown up without ceremony. Streets wider than before the war and more extensive squares were laid out. Expansive residential sectors were erected in record time, for which tens of thousands of Warsaw Robinsons were waiting. Large industrial establishments were built from their foundations, such as Warsaw had not had before the war.

But the rebuilding of the old historical sectors of the capital took place quite differently. Here something was done which a biographer of Warsaw wittily described as a "huge spiritualist séance." The spirit of a nonexistent city was summoned up from the other world, a city which for centuries had gradually grown in the course of years and had suddenly been shattered into ruins under the blows of the last war. At a time when a terrible lack of housing prevailed throughout Warsaw, and it was not possible in any way to satisfy the requirements of

Warsaw today. The East Wall

builders, then the best Warsaw architects, the most eminent sculptors and conservers of historical monuments pored over old plans and photographs and followed them, detail after detail, reconstructing the historical old houses of the Old and New Cities, as well as the splendid magnates' palaces in Cracow Boulevard. Such behavior must have seemed absurd to any foreigner. But the people of Warsaw approved wholeheartedly—even those who were nested at that time in conditions outraging the most primitive demands of civilization.

In present-day Warsaw there is now almost no trace of the war's destruction. The city is constantly being built up and extending into new districts. It is the heart and brain of Poland.

Party headquarters government building. Warsaw

Here, in the buildings of the Central Communist Party authorities and government are decided the directives which shape
the present and future of the country. Here are the main centers of cultural and scientific life as well as large industrial establishments. In the old magnates' palaces are located the ministries, artistic academies, scientific institutions and museums.
The reconstructed historical sectors are already covered with a
venerable patina of time and it is hard to imagine that there
has been a pause of several years in their age-old life stories.

Every day numerous excursions from Poland and abroad
visit the capital. As is usual, the tourists are most interested in
historical monuments. Wandering around the stylish little
streets and markets of the Old and New Cities, looking at the

majestic palaces and churches, they listen eagerly to the accounts by their guides of old-time kings and heroes, and also of the heroes of the last war who spun a new legend for the historical areas of Warsaw.

But no one tells these tourists of the nameless and ineffective heroism of the ordinary patriots of Warsaw, who squeezed voluntary offerings from their modest budgets during the hardest times and voluntarily prolonged their housing Robinsonade just to resurrect the historical beauty of their native city. And yet they also deserve a star in a Warsaw guidebook.

Many books about Warsaw have appeared since the war. The first of them bore the title *The Undefeated City*. This name has stuck to the Polish capital like a nickname. And rightly too.

THE CAPITAL OF KINGS

EVERY DAY AT NOON all the radio stations of the Polish Radio broadcast a solemn trumpet call. This is the famous Cracow *hejnal*. In beautiful old Cracow—formerly the capital of the Polish kings—the majestic Mariacki church stands in the central marketplace. Every hour the town trumpeter climbs up its lofty tower in order to resound this melodious time signal to all four corners of the world. Thanks to the invention of radio, the Cracow *hejnal* becomes the property of all Poland once a day. It is to be heard everywhere. It resounds from street loudspeakers and from the open windows of houses. Tourists traveling by car set their watches by it, as do holidaymakers sunbathing on beaches along the Baltic and people taking part in mountain climbing in the Tatras. The Poles are so used to their beloved *hejnal* that they do not notice a certain irregularity in its tune: the *hejnal* does not end harmoniously, but breaks off suddenly, as though the trumpeter were out of breath. Old chroniclers tried to explain this irregularity in the *hejnal*. Legend traces it from the Middle Ages, from the times of the Tartar invasions on Poland. One day troops of the slit-eyed riders penetrated to the walls of Cracow. The first to see them was the trumpeter on the Mariacki church tower. He pressed the trumpet to his lips (the *hejnal* was used exclusively as a warning in those days) to warn the town of the approach-

Trumpeter in a tower sounds the hejnal

ing danger. But the unfortunate man did not have time to finish, as an arrow from a Tartar bow penetrated his throat. The *hejnal,* interrupted in this dramatic manner, has remained thus ever since. For Cracow respects historic traditions.

Yes, the former capital of the kings of Poland respects and loves the traditions of its age-old luster. Like Florence, in Italy, Cracow does not conceal her historic souvenirs in the closed rooms of museums, but places them ostentatiously on show and allows every passerby in the streets to be familiar with them every day. Walking around the streets and squares of Cracow you have to stop every few moments to feast your eyes on some particularly beautiful monument of Gothic or Renaissance architecture. And on every such occasion, willy-nilly, you have to study the history of Poland.

Barbican fortress, Cracow Gardens. Warsaw

The Cracow Gardens (Planty)—a huge open park—surrounds the entire historic city center with greenery. The red mass of a round fortress appears from behind the greenery, with graceful little towers jutting up. This is the famous Barbican, generally known here as the Rondel—one of the now few excellently preserved examples in Europe of medieval fortifications. It was from this brick fort, which today is located in the center of the city but which at one time was a projecting part of the defensive walls, that Tartar invasions were repulsed. During the five centuries of its existence, the Barbican resisted countless enemy sieges. If we were to describe them all on memorial inscriptions there would not be space for them on the walls of the massive building. This is why the inhabitants of Cracow chose only one incident from the history of the Barbican, perhaps not the most important, but striking for all that. Bricked into the east wall of the fortress is a tablet in memory of Marcin Oraczewicz, a Cracow craftsman who in 1768 shot the leader of troops besieging the town with a jacket button loaded into his rifle.

The Gothic Collegium Maius is the oldest university building preserved in Poland. It is one of the buildings of the Jagiellonian University, which celebrated the six hundredth year of its existence in 1963–64. The most eminent representatives of culture and science from many countries traveled here for the jubilee celebrations. This is not surprising. The Jagiellonian University is one of the oldest and most respected places of learning in the world. Early in the sixteenth century, the most celebrated Polish astronomer, Nicholas (Mikolaj) Copernicus, studied here; he was the man who "stopped the sun and started the earth moving," thus creating the basis of modern astronomy. The scholar Paul (Pawel) Wlodkowicz was a professor at this university; he was sent as the Polish king's ambassador to the council at Constance (1414–18) and amazed the rulers gathered there with his demands that nobody had the right to occupy other countries or to spread religious beliefs by force. At a time when religious wars were being fought over most of Europe, and when dissenters from the prevailing faith were persecuted, reformers from England, Germany, Bohemia and France uttered their "heretical" views freely from the beautiful galleries of the Collegium Maius. The light of tolerance radiating from this place of learning drew repressed intellectuals to Cracow from all parts of the world.

In November 1939 the Nazis closed the Cracow university and arrested its professors. After savage beatings, the scholars were deported to a concentration camp in Sachsenhausen Oranienburg, from which many of them never returned. This unheard-of act of violence hastened the organizing of the underground resistance movement throughout the entire country

Celebration at the 6ooth anniversary of the Jagiellonian University

Central marketplace. Cracow

against the invaders, which lasted until the end of the occupation.

Most of the historical monuments of Cracow are gathered around the central marketplace, in which stands the Mariacki church already mentioned. The marketplace is surrounded by old palaces and houses dating from the fourteenth, fifteenth and sixteenth centuries, carefully restored by postwar architects and artists. Important events, exerting an influence on the fate of the nation, took place in almost every one of these buildings. Famous leaders and politicians, great scholars and artists lived in them. In the Wierzynek building—well-known to present-day tourists for its excellent restaurant—the wealthy citizen of Cracow Nicholas (Mikolaj) Wierzynek received a gathering of European monarchs at a splendid banquet. They had been invited to Cracow by King Kazimierz (Casimir) the Great, of the Piast dynasty.

A long, two-storied building in the finest Renaissance style divides the marketplace into two parts. This curious architectural monument—probably the only one of its kind in the world—is called the Cloth Hall and it records the location of the medieval trading center of Cracow. During the centuries, the Cloth Hall has frequently changed shape and appearance, but lively trading has continued in it unchanged for seven hundred years. The present-day customer in the Cloth Hall, buying a Cracow souvenir in the stores or stalls of the Central Office of Folk and Artistic Industry, realizes with gratification that once on this very spot medieval knights in armor made purchases, as did pretty town girls in high white coifs and courtiers of the most celebrated Polish kings.

Close by the Cloth Hall two tablets walled into the pavement of the marketplace bear witness to great deeds of the past. The tablet on the southern side informs us that on this spot on April 10, 1525, the king of Poland Zygmunt the Old of the Jagiellonian dynasty, seated on his throne, received the vassal tribute from Prince Albrecht Hohenzollern, kneeling at his feet. The prince was the last Grand Master of the defeated Teutonic Knights. This was a joyful day for Cracow and the entire country. Poland's eternal and most dangerous enemy had changed into her obedient vassal. Unfortunately, the strange course of our history has meant that 270 years later the heir of that kneeling vassal, King Frederick Wilhelm II Hohenzollern of Prussia, penetrated to the capital of the Polish state as one of its three partitioners.

The tablet on the other side of the Cloth Hall indicates the spot from which, in March 1794, Tadeusz Kosciuszko, leader of the insurrection, solemnly vowed to the nation to liberate it from foreign dominance. To stress the independent and republican nature of the insurrection, Kosciuszko that day wore the uniform of an American general, which he had worn several years earlier when fighting for the independence of the United States.

In the evening, when an old lamplighter lights the last gas lamps in Cracow in the arcades of the Cloth Hall, the marketplace takes on a special charm. It becomes something in a fairy tale. Mysterious shadows start wandering in the arcaded walls of the old buildings. The curious stone masks adorning the Renaissance roof of the Cloth Hall come to life. Moonlight gilds the crown on the Mariacki tower. And from beneath the crown, the melody of the medieval bugle resounds. Guides like to bring foreign tourists here in the evenings and scare them with tales of Master Twardowski, a legendary Polish wizard sent by the devil to the moon. At this hour a faithful servant of Twardowski is supposed to let him down to the marketplace changed into a spider on a long silver thread to collect for his master the latest Cracow gossip. This legend has many believers among the youngest children of Cracow. Little people of Cracow, attentively following TV reports of cosmic flights, have the right to ask what the first men on the moon will do when they find two Poles there already—Twardowski and his servant.

A few hundred yards from the marketplace, an impressive collection of historic buildings patronizes the city from a steep cliff over the Vistula. From the massive bastions, lofty steep roofs and filigree towers covered by time with a green patina, there radiates regal majesty. This is the Wawel, the most splendid and valuable of the Cracow monuments, dear to the heart of all Poles, the former seat of the Piast and Jagiellonian dynasties, the Pantheon of the Polish nation.

For four centuries, Polish monarchs rebuilt and converted their main residence. This is reflected in the variety of styles

The Wawel. Cracow

which characterizes the extensive complex of the Wawel's buildings. Here all the periods of royal Poland get along together in perfect harmony. Alongside the lofty medieval cathedral shines the pure gold dome of the marvelously sculptured sixteenth-century chapel. Alongside the ancient seat of the Piasts, a Gothic castle with plain walls and a steep roof, the splendid palace of the last Jagiellonians expands its Renaissance charm.

Almost all the kings of Poland are buried in the vaults of the Wawel cathedral, including those who ruled in Warsaw. Their adorned tombs, sculptured by famous artists of various periods, stand in the naves of the cathedral and in adjoining chapels. A walk through this mausoleum of rulers is very in-

Art treasures in the Hall of Deputies, the Wawel. Cracow

structive. You can learn from the guides how strangely the historical destiny of Poland worked out, and the cause of this.

Here, carved in red marble, is the tomb of the last king of the Piasts, Kazimierz the Great. The old bearded king, wearing a crown, rests on a monumental Gothic sarcophagus. He was one of the most eminent rulers of Poland. He finally consolidated the state, which had for some time been split in feudal districts of the quarreling Piasts. The king laid down wise laws and strengthened his defenses. He held a tight rein on the magnates and gentry, and supported the oppressed classes—townspeople and peasants. Thanks to this, general prosperity increased during his rule, crafts, trade and building developed, and culture flourished. The gentry of the time ironically called him "king of the peasants," but history has given him the title Great. Unfortunately Kazimierz left no male heir. The native dynasty of the Piasts, which had ruled Poland for four centuries, ended with this wise, just and economical ruler. The vacant throne in Cracow was taken over by monarchs of foreign origin.

Here are two more tombs deserving particular attention: that of Queen Jadwiga of the Hungarian dynasty of the Andegavens and that of her husband, King Wladyslaw Jagiello, of the Lithuanian dynasty. The wedding of these two directed the history of Poland into entirely new lines.

Jadwiga, a Hungarian princess and niece of Kazimierz the Great, was brought to the Wawel and crowned ruler of Poland when she was barely thirteen. Two years later, yielding to the persuasion of officials of the kingdom, she married the almost forty-year-old Jagiello, heir of the Great Kingdom of Lithuania. The lords of Cracow, in calling Jagiello to the throne and in this way carrying out a dynastic union between two neighboring countries, were acting in accordance with the best interests of the Polish state, as well as with their own. The state of Lithuania was at that time several times larger than Poland, since it included the lands of several Russian kingdoms incorporated previously; so it was important as an ally in the struggle with the common enemy, the Teutonic Knights. On the other hand, the primitive backwardness of most of the Jagiello territories created unusually favorable conditions for Poland to expand politically, economically and culturally, and the Polish magnates intended primarily to benefit from this expansion.

The figure of Queen Jadwiga is surrounded in Poland with unusual respect. Many literary works have been devoted to her and many romantic legends are told of her. Apparently she long refused to marry the older Jagiello, for she longed for a young Austrian prince who had been destined to marry her while she was still a child. A gate is still shown in the Wawel

The sarcophagus of Kazimierz the Great, the Wawel. Cracow

upon which the girl queen hurled herself with an ax, to make a way to her beloved. In the end, however, she yielded her feelings to her royal duties. To her also is attributed the joining of the two kingdoms and the collective christening of pagan Lithuania (the Russian territories which were in the Lithuanian state had become Christian much earlier, but from the East and according to the Greek Orthodox rite). Jadwiga died young and childless. In her will, she left a large part of her personal fortune for the development of the Cracow Academy, later called the Jagiellonian University.

King Wladyslaw Jagiello has gone down in the pages of the history of Europe for a splendid victory over the Teutonic Knights in the battle of Grunwald—one of the greatest battles of the Middle Ages. After the death of Jadwiga he married again three times. Not until his fourth marriage, with the Russian princess Sonka Holszanska—when he was already eighty— did he have two sons. Thanks to them he became the founder of a new royal Polish dynasty of Russian and Lithuanian origins—the Jagiellos.

A long row of Wawel tombs marks the more than 150-year rule in Cracow of the descendants of Jagiello—kings of Poland and Lithuanian princes. They were kings in the full sense of that word. Through extensive connections by marriage with other European dynasties, they became one of the most powerful families of monarchs in the world. Some of them also took their places on the thrones of Bohemia and Hungary. After the submission of the Teutonic Knights, the huge Polish-Lithuanian kingdom reached from the Baltic in the north to the Black Sea in the south, and in the east it reached almost as far as Moscow.

As regards politics and culture, the rule of the Jagiellos is generally considered the finest period of Polish history. They elevated Poland to the rank of a great European monarchy. The magnificence of their court and the flourishing of the uni-

Sarcophagus of Queen Jadwiga, the Wawel. Cracow

versity which they founded made Cracow an unusually attractive place for the intellectual and artistic elite of the whole civilized world. As educated people, they patronized all the sciences and arts. In their time the astronomer Nicholas Copernicus made many of his memorable discoveries, the great historian Jan Dlugosz composed his *History of the Polish Nation*, the genius Wit Stwosz sculpted wonderful altars and Cracow monuments, while the "fathers of Polish poetry and prose," Jan Kochanowski and Nicholas Rej, created works of literature which live to this day. The splendid cultural inheritance of these times fully justifies the name traditionally given them of the "Golden Age."

But the germs of all later weaknesses and defeats and of final collapse were already rooted in this great, powerful and enlightened Jagiellonian state. The Jagiellos departed from the wise policy of balance between social classes adopted by Kazimierz the Great. In the struggle with the magnates for strengthening the young dynasty on the throne, they leaned entirely on the gentry class. Loaded with privileges, the gentry soon became the ruling element in the state. But the other side of every new privilege for the gentry was restriction of the rights of townspeople and peasants. In the second half of the rule of the Jagiellos, Polish towns which had flourished under Kazimierz the Great began declining, and the social situation of the farming population in the country underwent a decided worsening.

There were other errors too. Despite the submission of the Teutonic Knights in Prussia on the Baltic, the Jagiellos did not have the heart to drive out the German dynasty ruling there, probably because the Prussian Hohenzollerns were related to them. The consequences of this were disastrous. When the Baltic line of the Hohenzollerns died out (this occurred after the last Jagiellos), their Berlin cousins, the Brandenburg Hohenzollerns, took over rule on the Baltic. They were later the kings of Prussia and German emperors, and held Poland in iron claws on the west and north, thus creating for the next three hundred years an excellent base for all kinds of provocative activities.

It was also difficult for the Jagiellos to carry through to the end the complex tasks resulting from the many-nation character of this extensive kingdom. The cementing of the huge state was only superficial. The internal policies of the Jagiellos encouraged the rapid Polonization of the Lithuanian magnates and gentry. Meanwhile, the peasants and townspeople—particularly in Belorussia and the Ukraine—kept their national separateness, which was underlined too by their different religion.

Furthermore, the powerful empire of Muscovy was growing along the eastern frontiers of the united Polish-Lithuanian state, aiming to draw under its rule all the former Russian territories. Sooner or later this had to lead to serious conflicts.

Thus, when the Golden Age of Polish history came to an end and the famous Jagiellonian dynasty died out, its successors on the throne took over a state of really impressive dimensions, but with frontiers threatened from the west, north and east, not solidified internally but rather at the mercy of one social class. Only very strong royal authority could have regulated and made healthy such a difficult inheritance. But after the Jagiellos there were no more strong kings on the throne of Poland.

After the disappearance of the dynasty, the gentry class, which the Jagiellos had elevated, became the real ruler of the state. All the gentry henceforward elected each successive king by means of what was called "free election."

Some of the elected monarchs subjected Polish policies entirely to foreign dynastic interests. The Frenchman Henri de Valois fled secretly from Poland on hearing of the death of his brother, and made the country the laughingstock of Europe. The event was celebrated by a satirical poem which circulated widely in Europe (in Latin) and mocked Poland. Two Swedes of the Vasa dynasty, embroiled in a struggle for the family crown, entangled Poland in a long war with Sweden and brought about bloody Cossack rebellions in the Ukraine. Germans of the Saxon dynasty of Wettin brought the Polish-Lithuanian state to a condition of total anarchy and ruin as a result of their political machinations.

All the same, truly outstanding rulers occurred amid the elected kings too, with excellent politicians in their chanceries and great leaders at the head of their armies. Suffice it mention Stefan Batory, a Hungarian; Wladyslaw IV, a Swede; and Jan III Sobieski, a Pole and famous defender of Europe from the Turkish deluge. But none of them was able to avert or slow

Sarcophagus of the Vasa kings, Chapel of Zygmunt. Cracow

down the evils resulting from the faulty internal system of the great state.

Each elected king of Poland had to confirm all their former privileges to his noble electors and vow to give them new ones, since his election depended on this. After the Jagiellonian Golden Age came two centuries of the gentry's "golden liberty." The most harmful creation of this period was the institution known as the *liberum veto,* according to which every gentry deputy to the Sejm (and there were no other deputies in the Polish Sejm) could simply shout "I forbid" and interrupt the Sejm deliberations, thus rendering impossible the functioning of the highest lawgiving authority of the state. Under such conditions it was difficult to rule the "gentry republic" and still more difficult to carry out any kind of reforms restricting the rights of the gentry.

The principal slogan of "golden liberty" was expressed in the phrase: "A gentleman on his farm is the equal of the palatine." This meant that the poorest "gentleman" could take part in ruling the country just like the most powerful magnate. But it was a lying slogan. The crowds of gentry, electing their kings and overturning the Sejm, governed only in appearance. Behind them stood the magnates who directed the gentry, buying them in all sorts of ways.

In the course of time, the magnates grew increasingly independent of the royal authority. It was they who decided the results of elections, overturning Sejms by gentry deputies they bribed, carrying on their own foreign policies, and forming armed confederacies against any authority seeking to restrict their liberties, using in this the help of neighboring powers. The throne of the Piasts and Jagiellos became a playing card in a game between groups of quarreling princelings. More than once it happened that two elected kings emerged from the elections, which in turn led to long and destructive civil wars with foreign soldiers taking part. And it should be remembered that this happened in times when hereditary royal dynasties were forming in countries neighboring on Poland, tightly holding the entire state authority in their own hands.

Political chaos brought economic ruin with it. The fortunes of individual magnates amounted to the dimensions of separate small states, but the towns deteriorated—deprived of laws, destroyed by incessant wars—and the peasantry sank into ever increasing enslavement. National conflicts on the territories of the Great Kingdom of Lithuania intensified. Because the Polish element there was almost entirely the landowning and official classes, the relationship of the local Lithuanian, White Russian and Ukrainian population with their Polish fellow citizens became an increasingly reluctant and often hostile dependence of subjects on their masters.

All this together could not help but lead to disaster. During the rule of the last king, Stanislas Poniatowski, and already after the first partition of the state, a group of enlightened magnates and progressive gentry activists finally succeeded in forcing through basic reforms in the system. This occurred in the Sejm which lasted four years and has gone down in history as the Great Sejm. For a short time the sun of the May 3, 1791, Constitution shone over the unfortunate country. It was one of the wisest and most progressive constitutional resolutions of those times. But three powerful monarchies—Russia, Austria and Prussia, which had already seized sections of Poland—did not in the least want the country to be internally stronger. It was they who came forward in the defense of the gentry's "golden liberty," restricted by the new Constitution. And they defended it so effectively that they brought about the total liquidation of the gentry state. The remains of the last king of Poland, who favored great reforms but could not defend his country's independence, are not buried in the Wawel; they rest in foreign soil.

So much can be discovered about the greatness and decline

of Poland by wandering around the royal mausoleum on the Wawel hill. In addition to former rulers in the vaults of the Wawel, famous Poles whom the nation considered as "equal to kings" are also buried there. Here lie the two favorite Polish heroes: Tadeusz Kosciuszko and the brother-in-law of the last king, Prince Jozef Poniatowski, who tried by his praiseworthy life and heroic death to erase the stain from his family name. The two greatest Polish poets, Adam Mickiewicz and Juliusz Slowacki, also lie here. They lived at the same period as Byron and Pushkin, and were certainly no less talented than they. However, they have not become the property of readers throughout the world as Byron and Pushkin have. For they were spiritual guides of their nation during a period of enslavement, and their work was so closely associated with "strange Polish matters" that only Poles can understand them properly. There is also the last Wawel crypt, which is also the latest; in it rests the marshal of Poland, Jozef Pilsudski, the helmsman of the ship of state during the Second Republic.

It is not possible to describe here the art treasures and historical monuments located in the Wawel. That would need another book. Readers must be satisfied with the assurance that the splendidly arranged interiors of the Wawel arouse the same amazement in foreign visitors today as they did centuries ago.

Yet it very nearly came about that all these priceless treasures underwent irrevocable destruction. Before the Nazis left Cracow in January 1945, they prepared to blow the city up. They mined the Wawel, the Barbican and many other celebrated monuments.

A skillful tactical maneuver on the part of the approaching Soviet Army spared the historic city from annihilation. As a proof of gratitude, the City Council presented a diploma of honorary citizenship of Cracow to Marshal Ivan Koniev, commander of the southern front. Under the red walls of the

Barbican—from which in the eighteenth century a tsarist general was shot by a button—have remained the graves of young Soviet sappers who perished from Nazi mines while rescuing the Jagiellonian monument. In Poland, similar historic confrontations can be made at every step. So how can foreigners regard Poland as anything but a strange country?

Next to Warsaw, Cracow is the largest scientific and cultural center of the Polish People's Republic. As the city escaped destruction during the war, the continuity of its cultural heritage can be sensed distinctly. Cracow has its famous dynasties of scholars and artists, who have served for several generations in the university or created their own individual artistic style. The "Cracow school" of mathematics and the "Cracow school" of stage design are acquiring increasing recognition throughout the world.

Since the last war, the venerable but somewhat museumlike atmosphere of Cracow has undergone a renewal of vitality. A wit has said that Cracow grew older day by day before World War II, but since 1945, the city has grown younger day by day. This can best be observed in the spring, when the International Festival of Short Movies is held in the city, the streets are thronged by colorful, singing crowds of students, and traditional shows and entertainments take place in the Wawel castle and on the river Vistula. Then the old city of the Piasts and the Jagiellos boils over with youth.

Figures bear witness to the dynamic development of Cracow in the postwar years. At present the city has over half a million inhabitants, or twice as many as in 1939. The area of the city, enlarged by new residential and industrial districts, is five times the size of prewar Cracow. Higher education has also developed impressively. Before the war, Cracow had four high schools with less than 8,000 students. Today, there are

A group of highlanders on stage

eleven high schools with 32,000 students taking advantage of them.

This sudden return to youth and the heightened dynamism of the royal city—which before the war was already betraying symptoms of decay—have been brought about by an experiment started twenty years ago on the site of a small village eight miles from Cracow. But we shall consider this experiment in the next chapter. For the time being, in bidding farewell to Cracow, we should mention one of Poland's greatest painters, who lived and worked here toward the end of the last century.

Matejko's Hall, the National Museum. Grunwald

Jan Matejko (1838–93) devoted all his great talent to historical paintings. He created an uncountable number of huge canvases, commemorating the most important moments in Polish history. Each of these pictures, preceded by long and deep historical researches, gives such an impression that the pictures are unforgettable after only one viewing. Most of the works of Matejko which have survived are on public view in the museums of Cracow and Warsaw. But color reproductions of his most popular paintings, e.g., "Grunwald Battle," "Prussian Tribute," "Kosciuszko at Raclawice," "Constitution of May 3" and

"Fellowship of Polish Kings," printed in hundreds of thousands of copies over the last decades, are to be found in almost every Polish home. Every Pole visiting historical monuments sees King Zygmunt the Old seated on his throne and the Grand Master of the Teutonic Knights kneeling before him, and Tadeusz Kosciuszko taking the oath of loyalty to the nation, and crowds cheering in honor of the May 3 Constitution, and the pale face of the last king signing the partition of the state. Not in vain is it said that Matejko "shaped the historical imagination of the Poles." No other nation in the world has such a picturesque vision of its history. This too contributes to some degree to the strangeness of Poland.

IT STARTED AT WANDA'S MOUND

A CCORDING TO A VERY ANCIENT LEGEND, the founder of Cracow was Prince Krakus, also called Krak, who is supposed to have lived in the seventh or eighth century A.D., long before the official emergence of the Polish state. This mythical ruler of the Poles must have had considerable difficulties in building his capital, since one of the oldest Polish proverbs says "Cracow was not built in a day." This proverb has been amazingly popular among the Poles. If anyone insists that a radiator which is not working right be fixed as soon as possible, or is trying to have a telephone installed, or complains that some officer is taking too long to attend to his problem, he hears in reply "Cracow was not built in a day." Poles have a feeling for history, so, consoled by this argument, they wait patiently, comforting themselves with the thought that Prince Krak was in a much worse situation, since in addition to troubles of a technical and bureaucratic nature he was also bothered by a greedy dragon. This wild creature, obviously lost from some other epoch, had taken up residence in a cavern under the Wawel and had to have herds of cattle driven to it for food; otherwise it attacked people. Or at least this is what the Bishop of Cracow, Vincenty Kadlubek, the thirteenth-century Polish chronicler, affirms. He was the first to write down the entire tale, on the basis of a considerably earlier oral tradition.

Prince Krak's modest state income could not satisfy the dragon's greed, so he decided to slay the monster. He told his two sons to fill an ox's skin with sulphur and throw it to the dragon instead of its usual breakfast. The simple creature let itself be taken in. It devoured an enormous quantity of sulphur, which caused it to be so thirsty that it drank up half the Vistula (some people say this is why the river is much narrower at Cracow than at Warsaw), and then it burst from overdrinking.

But joy at being liberated from the dragon did not last long. Krak died soon afterward, and his two sons killed one another in a fight for the succession. Krak's beautiful daughter, Princess Wanda, took her place on the vacant throne. And new troubles started right away. The powerful German prince Rytogar fell in love with Wanda and set out with his army for Cracow in order to win the hand of the charming ruler and at the same time take over Polish territory as dowry. Then Wanda vowed to the gods (this happened in pagan times) that she would sacrifice her life to them if they would help her protect her homeland from foreign invasion. The gods agreed to this arrangement and Wanda, at the head of the people of Cracow, wiped out Rytogar's army with the help of the gods and forced him to flee, after which, true to her vow, she drowned herself in the Vistula.

No one knows whether this legend has any factual background, yet Cracow traditions associate certain specific monuments with it. A large and deep hole has been preserved on the western slope of the Wawel hill, which has been known as the Dragon's Hole from time immemorial. The Krakus Mound dominates the Cracow Podgorze district: this is an old Slavic burial mound, considered to be the grave of the town's founder. Another similar mound, the Mound of Wanda, rises eight miles from Cracow, at the point where the Dlubna stream flows into the Vistula. At the foot of Wanda's Mound is located (or was until recently) the village of Mogila ("Grave"), commemorating by its name (supposedly) the suicide of the princess "who refused to marry a German."*

It was in the village of Mogila in 1949 that an undertaking of unusual importance for the entire country and especially for the county and province of Cracow was started.

Until 1949, Mogila had been a typical old village near Cracow. Now, after the changes in the economic structure of Poland, few such villages are left, and those that survive are more of a monument or reservation. But all their charms can be admired on the canvases of Cracow painters of the end of the last century. They have a sandy road planted with old willows, wooden huts deeply sunk into the ground, with walls painted blue or with white lime, and with high roofs of blackened straw. There are colorful flower beds under the windows and wells in the yards with high wooden shadoofs. These villages were very picturesque to look at, so students from the Cracow Academy of Fine Arts gladly came to them for the "fresh air," and foreign tourists traveling by automobile were delighted with "Polish exoticism."

But an unhappy way of life, totally without a future, was concealed behind this picturesque scenery. Time passed, yet the villages near Cracow seemed not to notice. Almost none of the advantages of civilization reached them. There was no electricity, no gas, no agricultural machinery or communication with the city. The poorer peasant farms, as a result of being continually handed down and split up among the heirs, became smaller and smaller. They looked impressive from the air, like a large carpet woven of narrow, varicolored strips. But for

* Words from an old folk song about Wanda. The song was so popular that even the emperor Napoleon learned it by heart during his battles in Poland.

Painted cottage near Cracow

the local farmers, who did not travel by air, and had to live on this land, they were less impressive.

It was more and more difficult for the large peasant families to live by working the parceled-out properties. More and more people had to leave their family plots of land and seek bread elsewhere. Some of them hired themselves out as laborers to rich landowners, some went to do farm work on local properties, most of them left the villages entirely in search of work. But it was not easy to get work in the cities either. Before the war, Cracow province was one of the least industrialized regions of Poland. Cracow itself, with its splendid cultural and scholarly center, had no industrial base and was reminiscent of a man with a large head on feeble little body. In this situation, the most enterprising peasants decided to seek work abroad. This did not happen in the Cracow region alone. The emigration of Polish peasants in search of work was occurring all over the country, and attained massive dimensions in the last years of the nineteenth century. During the Second Republic it was not possible to prevent this phenomenon, as its basic causes continued to exist, i.e., continually increasing overpopulation of the countryside and the slow tempo of industrial development. Peasant emigration for work was of two kinds: seasonal, for a few months of farm work, mainly to central and eastern Germany (from which the term "a trip to Saxony" survives to the present in Polish); or permanent, mainly to the United States and South America.

The dramatic fate of peasants forced by poverty to leave their homeland found wide reflection in Polish literature. Henry K. Sienkiewicz devoted his celebrated tale *For Bread* to it, the great poet Maria Konopnicka wrote a poetic tale called *Mr. Balcer in Brazil.* Many books about the peasant emigration appeared in the years before the war. Special fame was gained by the *Memoirs of Peasants* and *Memoirs of Emigrants,* compiled by sociologists.

The largest wave of peasant emigration abroad came from the economically backward provinces of southern Poland, with Cracow province among them. Even today, without any need of considering prewar statistics, it is easy to see this. It is precisely to these regions that most packages and letters from relatives in America come, and most foreign tourists of Polish origin stay here, coming every year to Gdynia on the transatlantic ship *Stefan Batory.*

Last year an elderly lady who looked like a foreigner came in a fine automobile to one of the villages near Cracow. Her

Polish liner Stefan Batory *sails for Montreal, Canada*

Polish lawyer accompanied her. The curious villagers were able to learn from him that his client was a rich American woman from Ohio and was interested, for reasons unknown to him, in this particular village. The lady spoke English to her lawyer and did not show any desire to make contact with the local population. But it was obvious she did not feel foreign in the village. Without asking the way, she at once set off in the direction of the state farm located on the site of an earlier manor and farm buildings. The sensational rumor spread through the village that the foreign woman was a relative of the prewar owner and had come to claim legally the return of the nationalized estate.

But the American woman was not at all interested in the manor of the expropriated landowner. Her entire attention was focused on the poorest of the farm buildings. It was a wooden shed, falling down with age, already marked for demolition, but still temporarily used as a tool shed. The foreign woman informed her lawyer that she wanted to buy this very building. The startled lawyer tried in vain to talk her out of it, explaining that a private individual could not buy property belonging to the state farm. The American woman insisted: she must have the shed and would pay any price for it. This was why she had come from Ohio.

Then the truth came out. The supposed foreigner had been born in a poor family with many children in a local village. As a young girl she had been sent to the manor as a servant. And in this same wretched shed—the living quarters of farm workers at that time—she had spent several of the hardest years of her life. When she emigrated, she vowed that when she made money abroad, she would buy this accursed shed on purpose to pull it down and build a "human" house on the site of her former wretchedness. She was fortunate beyond all expectation in the United States. Out of many thousands of emigrants, she was one upon whom fortune smiled: her husband found oil on his farm, or something of the sort. So, after over forty years, she returned to her native region to carry out her youthful vow. We do not know how the incident ended; possibly the negotiations for the purchase of the shed are still going on, for the citizen from Ohio gave the impression of being an energetic and stubborn person. In any case, it is worth remembering this typical incident, since it reminds us of the fate of village young people in the economically backward counties of prewar Poland.

After the war, agricultural reform changed the situation in the countryside. Great property holdings underwent expropriation. The land was divided out among many landless peasants; many parceled-out farms were merged and added to; industrialized state farms arose on the site of former private farms; state machinery centers and agricultural circles were formed to help poorer farmers, who were encouraged to join in production co-operatives. But all this did not suffice to give sufficient employment to the overcrowded villages around Cracow or to prevent renewed parceling out of farms. For there were still no large industrial enterprises in the neighborhood.

So when in 1949, after the rebuilding of the most important war damage, a start was made on carrying out large-scale plans for the industrialization of the country and it was planned to build, with Soviet help, a large combine of steel production and a town of a hundred thousand connected with it, the village of Mogila at the foot of the Mound of Wanda was chosen as the starting point of this first great socialist construction.

The deafening rumble of tractors, of great excavators, road machinery and trucks loaded with bricks and planks interrupted the stagnant hush of Cracow province. Staffs of experts trained during a three-year period of rebuilding were hastily mobilized in the ministries. Plans for the first districts of the future town were drawn in Warsaw and Cracow planning offices. Plans of the combine itself, according to agreements made, were to be supplied from Moscow. As a result of a mobilizing campaign, candidates for builders began coming to Mogila. Among them were eager volunteers from youth organizations, mistrustful peasants from neighboring villages, building workers dissatisfied with their work, lovers of adventure and ordinary adventurers, professional toughs and various sorts of black sheep.

The building of the combine and the city of Nowa Huta started in the late summer of 1949. On the area of the planned investment there still waved ripe corn. As the national press was conjuring up for its readers visions of great factories and the hundred-thousand city of workers, the future builders were industriously harvesting the corn alongside its astounded own-

Harvesttime on a state farm

ers. Not until the harvest was in did they start digging the foundations for the first homes. Little shepherd boys watched with interest from the hills intended to be the center of the combine. The incessant mooing of cows took the place of factory sirens for the time being. This was how it started.

In the rest of the world—in rich and highly industrialized countries, investments equally large and even larger are carried out and no special fuss is made on that account. But Poland was not a rich country, nor highly industrialized. The size and tempo of the planned enterprise had no precedence in the previous history of our building industry. Destroyed materially and biologically, society was only just recovering from postwar convalescence. The lack of professional skills was painfully

The Mazowsze plain. Farmland

felt in all areas. People were terribly weary after their experiences in the occupation and the three-year rebuilding. The international situation did not promise rapid settlement. Mysterious dramas, incomprehensible to most citizens, were being enacted in the world labor movement and in the Polish political leadership. Well-known names disappeared from the newspapers. Innocent people were sent to jail. The political battle was intensifying and the atmosphere of suspicion thickened.

The first great investment of the socialist plan for the building up of Poland, started under such conditions, was reminiscent of a complicated strategic operation carried out on many fronts by armies of untrained recruits led by officers of little experience. Everything began from the very beginning, every-thing had to be learned through mistakes and defeats, every-thing had to be hard fought for. People fought for the extension of railroads, for changing the course of rivers, for new bridges, railroads and highways, for building materials, water, coal, houses and clubs for the workers. They fought against their own lack of experience, the bureaucratic inertia of offices, ordinary human stupidity and malice, the weight of the past and new, harmful faults.

Nothing of all this was described in the newspapers, in order not to weaken the enthusiasm of the population for the great enterprise and "give food to enemies of the regime." Instead, mild articles were published about the town growing amid fields, the great advance of the neighborhood, peasants changing into a new working class, the people who were build-ing Nowa Huta and who would become citizens of a socialist city and workers in the huge combine. The smooth propa-ganda slogan was: "New walls are growing in Nowa Huta, and new people along with the walls."

But events at Wanda's Mound did not develop as harmoni-ously as the slogan. The fragments of the prehistory of Nowa Huta, preserved in human memory, are full of dramatic inci-dents. Old Cracow adopted an attitude of dislike toward Nowa Huta at first. Fears were expressed that an industrial giant in the immediate neighborhood might damage the historical mon-uments, that the sudden influx of a new population would cause famine in the city of the Wawel. The countryside also treated the building suspiciously. There was a great deal of trouble with the owners of the lands expropriated on behalf of the future town. Some people moved without resisting to sub-stitute farms, mostly in the Western Territories of Poland, others took compensation in money and applied without much en-thusiasm for work in the building, but it also often happened that people dug themselves into their huts as if they were fortresses and desperately defended their old peasant poverty until the great building came up to their fences.

A plague of the first period was mass desertions from the site. These were caused by various things. Professional tramps vanished immediately after receiving working clothes and their first wages. Seasonal farm workers could not always get used to the difficulties of their new and unknown work, to the thick yellow mud which was often knee-deep and to the pitiful conditions of existence of the first builders. Deserters of both categories spread rumors which caused panic in the neighboring villages, rendering difficult the enrollment of new workers. Sometimes supernatural forces interfered with the building. A majestic Cistercian monastery was in the neighborhood of the village of Mogila (today it is the only historical monument of the city of Nowa Huta). The monastery was very old, as it is known from history that a radical social and religious reformer of the mid-fourteenth century, Fr. Galka of Dobczye, and a professor of the Cracow academy were imprisoned in it. As the Cistercian monks had got along very well for five hundred years without any great industrial enterprise, it was hard to expect them to be particularly friendly toward the socialist building site. And they had great influence on the peasantry. The entire district knew the story of the "gray monk"—one of the former priors of the monastery whose spirit appeared by night in places where a misfortune was about to occur. And in the early period the gray monk made the building site his favorite area for nocturnal walks. A certain laborer of Mogila who had insomnia used to see him at least once a week. These nocturnal visits influenced uneducated minds. The more superstitious peasants left the site secretly, without waiting for the misfortunes.

Once Nowa Huta was visited by a historical specter. It must be explained that the village of Mogila was located on the site of a battle of the Kosciuszko insurrection. Not far away was the famous Raclawice village, where General Tadeusz Kosciuszko at the head of peasant scythe bearers struck the tsarist General Tormasov on the head on April 4, 1794. The incident in Nowa Huta happened on April 4 when the first machinery from the Soviet Union was brought to the building site. The meeting of Soviet specialists and Polish engineers took place in a temporary field office located in an old peasant hut. Several building workers and laborers were discussing plans. Suddenly a young technician burst into the room like a bomb: "Listen!" he shouted without noticing the Soviet guests. "They say in the village that this was Kosciuszko's headquarters! The commander set off from this hut to Raclawice to fight the Muscovites!" An embarrassed silence fell in the office. The weight of 150 years of history was hanging over the heads of the representatives of the friendly nations. But the Russian engineers, when the matter was explained, adopted an attitude of proper distance to the historic conflict. There was talk of Kosciuszko for a while, then the interrupted working conference was started again. However, the news of the technician's gaffe spread widely through the site. Activists of a youth organization decided to interfere.

These young lads of Nowa Huta were splendid, or at least most if not all. Only five years younger than the generation which fought and died in occupation battles, they were in many ways reminiscent of them. They were just as enthusiastic and self-sacrificing, without any doubts of the rightness of their behavior and just as eager to perform great deeds for their homeland. But the previous generation had taken their models from Sienkiewicz's historical novels and Matejko's paintings, while these formed their view of the world on the basis of contemporary propaganda pamphlets and successive issues of the *Agitator's Notebook*. The previous generation gained their first fighting experience in armed actions against the Nazi occupiers, these in political battles for the realization of postwar socialist reforms.

Most of these young people came from the poorest huts of villages around Cracow. As children they had lived through all the horrors of war. Some had seen their closest relatives shot by the Nazis. Others had spent their childhood beside their parents in forced labor camps. Yet others, the most fortunate ones, had slipped for many months as messengers between their native villages and partisans' bivouacs hidden in the woods.

The new world—emerging from the chaos of war—was simple, comprehensible and full of promises to them. They had lost nothing and had everything to gain. The building of Nowa Huta was creating an unusual opportunity of social advance for them. They believed in it without any reservations and devoted themselves heart and soul to the great construction. It was precisely they who constituted the most self-sacrificial core of the building workers, from them were recruited the most fervent propagators of the new order. After the incident in the field office, they therefore set out to the workers' barracks to explain properly to the diggers from Mogila and other villages the turn of Polish history.

They spoke rapidly, enthusiastically, choking with emotion, about the common struggles of Polish and Russian revolutionaries against tsardom. They spoke of the fact that one of the first acts of the Soviet government after the Revolution had been the canceling of the act of partition of Poland. And of the thousands of Soviet soldiers who had died liberating Polish territories. Of the prospects of development of People's Poland. Referring to Kosciuszko's attitude toward the peasants, they presented the great investment near Cracow as the more daring realization of the reform plans of the "peasant leader." They assured their listeners that if Kosciuszko were still alive, he would have undoubtedly encouraged them to build Nowa Huta.

Terrible cold prevailed in the hastily erected barracks, and everything was covered with mud, as water had to be brought

A coal mine

half a mile. Deadly tired, the laborers grew furious with this "political chattering" which interrupted their well-deserved rest. Gazing at their working boots covered with a shell of yellow mud, they longingly thought of the warm smell of their family huts and the white walls on which, alongside holy pictures, hung the unchanging postcard reproductions of Matejko's painting "Kosciuszko at Raclawice." They could not for the life of them imagine the leader Kosciuszko as an agitator for Nowa Huta.

Much water has flowed down the Vistula since those days. Nowa Huta is already celebrating the twentieth year of its existence. On the hills alongside Wanda's Mound, where peasants' cows once mooed, the great furnaces of the Lenin combine breathe fire and steam. In 1969 the combine produced 4.3 million tons of steel, i.e., almost three times more than the average entire annual production of steel in prewar Poland.

The city of Nowa Huta, linked administratively with Cracow as its industrial district, now has around 150,000 inhabitants. Most of these are former peasants from villages around Cracow and other backward country regions. A sharp-witted sociologist could—on the basis of materials collected in almost every home in Nowa Huta—write an exciting study of the transformation of man under the influence of new living conditions. Such a work would tell of people who, before coming to Nowa Huta, often did not know how to read and write, had no qualifications, did not know the most elementary appliances. Today, the tenants of the houses of Nowa Huta are by a large majority qualified workers of large, modern industrial enterprises, and the young people coming from these houses are a large percentage of the students at Cracow's high schools. More and more people take advantage year by year of the libraries, reading rooms, House of Culture, theater, cinemas and other cultural arrangements. More and more radio sets, TVs, books, suites of furniture and reproductions of pictures are sold in the stores of Nowa Huta each year.

What started in 1949 at the Mound of Wanda spread throughout Poland and is going on today. In various places where coal, sulphur, copper, gas or other valuable raw materials have been discovered; where supplies of electrical energy hitherto not taken advantage of have been found in the courses of rivers; and primarily where empty blots could be seen on prewar economic maps—gigantic industrial settlements like Nowa Huta are growing, along with all its social and cultural results. Today Nowe Tychy, Turoszow, Plock, Konin, Oswiecim, Tarnobrzeg, Salina and many other places which before the war had nothing to do with industry or did not exist are named in the same breath as Nowa Huta. New industrial giants are built sometimes in bare fields, sometimes in the vicinity of big old cities, sometimes on the base of small, dying townships. But there are always similar difficulties and complications as at Wanda's Mound. With birth pangs and in the sweat of the brow, with difficulties and problems, at the cost of huge sacrifices and renunciations, the economic structure of the country and the social structure of the nation are changing.

As a result of the constant expansion of the economic basis, society is undergoing constant migratory processes. Every year tens of thousands of young peasants come to work in the cities. Every year tens of thousands of people move to new accommodations. Every year the circle of consumers of cultural goods widens. The number of schools, education and entertainment institutes, readers of books and magazines, owners of radio sets and TVs increases. New customs and a new mentality are forming. A new working class of peasant origins is still being created. The manner in which this class is brought up will decide the future of our country.

Nowa Huta, as the starting achievement of a great development, has almost symbolic significance. This is why visitors to

Modern housing at Nowa Huta

our country are most often taken there. Guides showing tourists around the new city like to end their account with the words "Cracow was not built in a day, but Nowa Huta was." This new proverb sounds rather lighthearted to a Polish ear. For every Pole knows well and feels how difficult it is to hasten on history.

LESSONS OF THE MILLENNIUM

O N FEBRUARY 25, 1958, the Sejm of the Polish People's Republic passed a solemn resolution announcing that the years 1960–66 would be the period of celebrating the millennium of the Polish state. For Poles, these celebrations became an opportunity for thorough study of their country's history.

The age of Poland was determined on the basis of many years of research. Historians and archaeologists found that in the years 960–66 the final union of the Slavic territories between the Oder and Bug rivers took place, under the rule of Prince Mieszko I of the Piast dynasty. From these years too come the first written mention of the existence of the Polish state, preserved in documents and chronicles of historians and travelers of the time. It is therefore recognized that the official written history of Poland amounts to a thousand years. This does not in the least mean that there was no state organization in our territories before that. Archaeological investigation shows that the first seeds of Polish statehood existed much earlier. (Around the third century a tribal state of Vislanians [Wislanie] existed in the southern Polish territories. The legend of Krak and Wanda is certainly associated with them. Later, the Vislanians were swallowed up by the Polanians [Polanie].) Every now and then in various parts of the country are found traces of defensive towns and settlements, and also a large number of various objects of daily use which prove that the inhabitants of these territories were already on a quite high level of civilization and social organization long before the year 960.

But we know very little about the times preceding this date. Only legends written down many years after certain events in Polish prehistory by the earliest Polish chronicler, Gall the Anonymous, writing at the beginning of the twelfth century, tell us of the events.

The oldest of these legends, known to every Polish child, tells of the dramatic circumstances accompanying the change of the ruling dynasty into the tribal state of the Polanians, which later developed into the Polish state; of the mournful end of the Popiel dynasty and the beginnings of the Piast dynasty.

The scene of these events was Gniezno in Greater Poland. (Although Poland has for fifty years been divided administratively into provinces, the historical names of former regions are still commonly used. So it is worth knowing that Gniezno and Poznan are in Greater Poland; Cracow in Little Poland; Warsaw in Mazovia; Katowice, Wroclaw and Opole in Silesia; and Danzig and Stettin on the Baltic coast.) Gniezno was at that time the capital of the Polanian state and later the first capital of the united Polish state.

At that time, Prince Popiel II sat on the throne of Gniezno. He was a stern and cruel ruler. He wanted to govern alone, without taking anyone's advice. His wife, a German, encouraged him in this, continually reminding him that this was the way princes ruled in Germany. However, the custom existed in Poland that the princes must take the advice of an assembly of older peasants or landowners in all more important matters. The assembly was known as a "rally." Popiel did not summon rallies and as a result came to disagree with the peasants, who refused to obey him and did not want to go to war with him. Popiel feared that his uncles would join with the rebellious peasants and deprive him of power. He invited his uncles to a banquet, and his wife gave them poisoned mead and wine, and killed them all. But punishment soon alighted on the wicked ruler. Thousands of mice emerged from the bodies of the murdered uncles and attacked the prince's court. Popiel fled from them to Kruszwica on Lake Goplo and took refuge in a tower built in the middle of the lake. However, the mice swam across, got into the tower and devoured the cruel prince (the tower in the Goplo still exists and is called the Tower of Mice).

So goes the first part of the legend, which is recorded in various versions by different chroniclers. The different versions do not agree in everything, but two moments recur in them unchanged: that Popiel was a wicked, cruel ruler, and that he died eaten by mice. Modern historians do not question the historical existence of the Popiel dynasty or its tragic end, but they refuse to believe in the mice. They therefore try to explain Popiel's death in a more realistic manner. One such explanation says that Popiel II was killed by the Mousians, the population of the village of Mouse, located not far from Kruszwica. However this may be, the Popiel legend has an optimistic sound for Poles and in various times of heavy oppression they have been supported by the hope that every wicked and cruel ruler must sooner or later come to a bad end.

The second part of the legend, about Piast, Popiel's successor on the Gniezno throne, is also encouraging. The chronicler Gall the Anonymous states that Piast was a frugal farmer and wheelwright in the service of the prince's court. His small but well-run farm was located in the borough of Gniezno, close to Popiel's seat. One day the same ceremony took place in the prince's castle and in the hut of his poor neighbor. It was the hair-clipping of the eldest son. This was an old Slavic rite based on transfer of the boy at the age of seven from the care of his mother to the rule of his father, who on this occasion cut with his own hands the boy's hitherto uncut hair.

At the peak of the ceremonies in Piast's house two young travelers appeared, to whom Popiel had refused hospitality in his court. Piast received them cordially, sharing with them everything he had, i.e., beer and the meat of one pig. For this the visitors blessed their host's son, young Ziemowit, promising to him and his descendants happy rule on the Polish throne, which probably no one present treated seriously. Soon afterward the well-known events happened to Popiel and the Polish peasants began gathering to a rally in Gniezno to elect a new prince. On the way they all dropped in on Piast's farm, as his wisdom, respectability and hospitality were known to all. The poor farmer worried what to serve so many venerable guests, but on looking into his larder he was surprised to see that it was filled with jugs of beer and hot pork. He at once understood that this miraculous increase in food and drink had occurred through the mysterious travelers he had received during the hair-clipping of Ziemowit. The peasants, delighted by the hospitality of the simple wheelwright, who was able to feed and give drink to so many people from his modest stores, decided that they would never find a better and more practical prince than Piast anywhere, and they led him to the vacant throne of Gniezno.

No one knows who these two mysterious travelers were who brought about the sudden enriching of Piast. The chronicler Gall does not try to explain them. Medieval interpreters of the legend saw them as the saints Cyril and Methodius, or angels from heaven. Present-day young people, preferring more up-to-date explanations, are inclined to consider them visitors from another planet. But people without imagination suppose that they were merely foreign emissaries who gave the future Polish ruler a disinterested loan. Because Poland never received dis-

interested foreign loans from anyone during her quite long
history, this third explanation must also be considered as
improbable as the two preceding ones. It is possible too that
these mysterious travelers simply did not exist, and the change
in dynasties took place under completely different circumstances. So it is not worthwhile paying any particular attention
to the matter. Of more importance is another element of the
Piast legend, viz. its unusually democractic nature. Apart from
the Czechs, the Poles are surely the one nation in world to
boast of the peasant origin of their kings.

Admittedly, later Polish historians have tried to take hold of
the wrong end of the stick, by supposing that "Piast" was not a
name but a high official of the court, a *piastun* ("guardian") or
educator of the heirs to the throne. The hypothesis had certain
likely elements, since somewhat earlier in the powerful state of
the Franks a similar court official overturned the ruling dynasty
of the Merovingians and became founder of the new dynasty of
the Carolingians. However, it must be remembered that the information about the creator of the Polish dynasty comes from
the chronicles of Gall the Anonymous, who was the court scribe
of Boleslas Wrymouth, a ruler coming in direct line from
Ziemowit, son of Piast. It is hard to suppose that the name and
origin of the prototype of the dynasty was not known at the
Polish court at the end of the eleventh century and that his
social status was deliberately degraded. In any case, Piast has
survived to the present in public opinion as a symbol of the
country folk. During the Second Republic, as many as two
peasant political parties chose Piast as their patron. Maybe the
democratic start of the dynasty also influenced the official
name of the state. Even under the rule of kings, Poland was a
"republic," and so the property of all. It is another matter that
the "all" at that time were the gentry. The name "Polish Republic," has lasted to postwar times. Not until the 1952 Constitution was the name changed to Polish People's Republic,
to stress that the working people are the stewards in the state.

The oldest Polish legends hand down to us two diametrically different kinds of rulers: the wicked, cruel tyrant Popiel, probably the descendant of foreign invaders (modern historians suppose that the Popiels came from Scandinavia), and the democratic, virtuous and practical native Piast. The Piast type and the Popiel type will often alternate with one another in the succeeding centuries of Polish history.

According to Gall the Anonymous, Prince Mieszko, the first historical ruler of Poland, was a grandson of Ziemowit, the son of Piast. The name of Prince Mieszko as ruler of the Polish state has been preserved in the chronicles of Thietmar, a German bishop, the Russian historian Nestor and the Arabic traveler Ibrahim ben Jacob.

Characteristically, the earliest mention in chronicles of the existence of the Polish state is connected with an attack on Poland by the German leader Wichman. This is all the more significant in that—as we know—"negative" characters in the two oldest Polish legends are also Germans: in the legend of Wanda, Prince Rytogar, and Popiel's wife. This is not mere coincidence, but a confirmation of the unhappy experiences which history has not spared the Poles. During the next thousand years of neighborhood with Germany, nothing but evil things resulted for Poland.

The writings of chroniclers contemporary with Mieszko I tell us of his marriage to the princess Dobrawa, the daughter and sister of Czech rulers. It was to Dobrawa that a decisive role in converting the Polish prince and his subjects to Christianity is attributed. The year 966 is generally considered to be the date of Poland's christening. From this date, the young Slavic state begins to be regarded as a full-fledged member of the civilized societies of the Europe of that time, and the German margraves and counts lurking on its frontiers lose their excuse for laying waste Polish territories with fire and sword, on the pretext of spreading Christianity. To facilitate the reader's locating the start of the Polish state in time, it can be related to other historical events. Princess Dobrawa came to Poland a hundred years before William the Conqueror landed in England, and Prince Mieszko I died five hundred years before Columbus discovered America.

During the celebration of the millennium, the period of Prince Mieszko and his great son Boleslas the Bold was the object of much attention, since it was precisely these two rulers who gathered under their dominion all the ethnically Polish territories. In the last years of Mieszko I, the extent of his state was almost indentical with the territory of People's Poland today. It is also worth remembering that he built two fortified towns: Danzig on the Baltic and Opole in Silesia. In giving a start to these cities, the ruler of Poland could not of course foresee the difficult conditions under which they would have to defend their Polish character against a German invasion a few centuries later.

Mieszko's son Boleslas the Bold, also called the Great by contemporaries, is regarded as Poland's greatest ruler. He was an excellent leader, a fine administrator and a farseeing politician. After his father's death he had to battle for a time for the throne with his mother-in-law and her three sons, who were supported by the Germans. However, he defeated his rivals and forced them to leave the country, by means of which he saved the unity of the Polish state, which he then ruled personally for thirty-three years.

By means of wise alliances, Boleslas tried to ensure Poland's security on the north, east and south, and concentrated all his attention on the west. The main aim of his policy was the liberation of all the Slavic lands held by the Germans and the creation of a great west Slavic state. He wanted to become totally independent of the German kings, who were also west Roman (Holy Roman) emperors and claimed feudal domination over all western Europe.

The behavior of the Roman-German emperor Otto III at the famous Gniezno assembly in the year 1000 bears witness to the seriousness with which the West regarded the ruler of Slavic Poland.

Otto III came to Gniezno on a pilgrimage to the grave of St. Wojciech, murdered three years before during missionary work in Prussia, neighboring on Poland. This Wojciech, a Czech prince and Bishop of Prague, was one of the most outstanding figures of his time. One day he renounced all spiritual and secular honors and decided to become a plain missionary monk. The aim of his life was to convert to Christianity pagan Prussians who lived in a country on the Baltic east of the Vistula mouth. It must be pointed out that the Prussians of that time, who came from the same family as the Lithuanians, had nothing in common with the German Prussians, who later on seized their country and name. Boleslas was very concerned with subjugating his primitive and warlike northern neighbors, but faithful to his western policy he did not want to seize their country by force. So he was very favorable toward Wojciech's peaceful mission, gave him an armed escort for his personal safety and facilitated his journey by sea from Polish Danzig to Prussia. He figured that the Prussians, after receiving Christianity from the hands of a Slavic missionary, would of their own free will enter into friendly relations with powerful Poland and would yield to her influence. We may suppose that the fates of the Prussians and Poland would have turned out quite differently if these calculations of the wise ruler had worked out. Alas, they did not. Wojciech, who trusted entirely in the power of his oratory and God's protection, sent Boleslas' escort away after reaching Prussia and set out for the depths of the country with only two companions. Soon afterward he perished by the spear of a Prussian warrior. Boleslas ransomed from the Prussians the body of the missionary for its weight in gold and solemnly buried him in Gniezno cathedral.

Wojciech's death caused a shock in all Western Christendom. Soon afterward the Pope canonized the martyr and the highest secular ruler of the Christian West set out on foot on a pilgrimage to his tomb.

The young German-Roman emperor, who was half Greek by birth but a Roman by education, did not dislike the Slavs as his predecessors and successors on the imperial throne had. Pleased by his splendid reception in Gniezno and the great personality of the Polish ruler, he took such a liking to him that he placed on Boleslas' head his own imperial crown and handed him the symbol of his own power, the spear of St. Maurice. Historians have not to this day been able to decide what this unusual gesture on the part of the highest ruler of feudal Europe indicated. Some suppose that Otto III appointed Boleslas an imperial patrician and his commander in the East, while others suppose that he selected him as his heir to the imperial throne. However this may be, this was surely the most cordial and disinterested gesture of a German ruler toward Poland for a thousand years of Polish-German relations.

Two years after the Gniezno assembly, the splendor and solemn atmosphere of which all contemporary chroniclers bear witness to, Emperor Otto III, favorably inclined to Poland, died at a young age. His successor, Emperor Henry II, has gone down in history as an unrelenting enemy of the Slavs, especially Poland. The later years of Boleslas' rule passed in constant wars with Germany. Poland emerged victorious from these wars and with greatly extended frontiers. The powerful and ethnically unified state of Boleslas reached from the Carpathians to the Baltic, from Szczecin to Danzig, from the Bug to the upper Laba. The last achievement of the magnificent rule of the great Piast was his coronation in 1025 as first king of Poland. This set the final seal on the total sovereignty of the youthful state.

A few months after his coronation, Boleslas died at the age

of nearly sixty. He was buried alongside his father in Poznan, the largest city in Greater Poland, which had become the capital of Poland during the reign of Mieszko I.

It is worth recalling a certain historical monument of the times of Boleslas. It is connected with his excursion to Kiev, undertaken not for aggressive purposes, but to return the throne to the legal ruler of that town who was allied to Poland, the Russian prince Swiatopelk. Riding into conquered Kiev, Boleslas struck his sword on the town gate in accordance with custom. The blow was so strong that the sword split. This split sword of the great Boleslas, named "the Split," was later the coronation sword of all Polish kings. Up to the last war, the sword reposed in the Wawel treasury. In September 1939 it was successfully taken abroad along with the priceless tapestries of the last Jagiellos.

After many adventures and wanderings, the venerable national monuments found themselves in Canada. For various reasons of a political and legal nature they remained there a very long time and only a few years ago were returned to Poland. Their return was celebrated throughout the country in a solemn holiday. Today Boleslas' sword occupies its proper place among the most valuable treasures of the Wawel.

After the splendid era of Mieszko and Boleslas, rulers who personified all the virtues of the legendary Piast, very hard times began for Poland. Surveying the gloomy chronicles of this period we have the impression that bloody Popiel was again ruling in Poland and, taking his revenge for his own decline, was destroying everything the great Piasts had done.

Boleslas' great work collapsed under the pressure of unequaled defeats. The three sons of the great king fought a fratricidal war for the throne. They drove each other out of the country, after which they came back supported by foreign troops. After seizing power, one of them—to spite his brother—sent back the crown won by his father to the German emperor,

Boleslas' sword, the Wawel. Cracow

depriving Poland by this gesture of its royal independence. All the decentralizing forces of the young state, suppressed by Mieszko and Boleslas, began functioning again. High officials and the descendants of former tribal princes took advantage of the weakening of the central power and tore the state into pieces, from which they created separate regions of their own. In reply to the growing violence of the aristocracy, bloody folk rebellions broke out, linked with a return to paganism. The rebellious peasants murdered their lords and bishops, wrecked Christian churches and set up altars on the ruins to old Slavic gods. Foreign German, Russian and Czech soldiers ran wild across the whole country. The two Piast capitals, Gniezno and Poznan, were destroyed.

A long time passed before the next ruler of Poland (uncrowned), Prince Kazimierz the Restorer (Casimir I), succeeded in bringing the country out of this unheard-of chaos and rebuilt a united state. But it was not until the Restorer's son, grandson of Boleslas, also named Boleslas, called "the Bold," ascended the throne that he returned her power and splendor to Poland.

The third eminent Piast on the Polish throne was reminiscent in some ways of his grandfather. Like the latter, he was a talented leader and sharp-witted politician. However, he had similar faults. He offended people by his pride and violent character, he was impetuous and frivolous. Apparently he lost Pomerania at the start of his reign by his recklessness. However, he succeeded in rebuilding strong state authority and in strengthening Poland's authority in Europe. Like Boleslas the Bold he aimed at entire independence from the emperor.

Boleslas the Bold ruled 1058–73. At that time Europe was experiencing dramatic events which were reflected in many later literary works. The two highest leaders of the Christian West, Pope Gregory VII Hildebrand and the emperor of the Holy Roman (German) Empire, Henry IV, were carrying on a bitter quarrel for the right to bestow Church offices (known as the "war of investiture"). European states were divided into two fighting camps. Boleslas, in accordance with his anti-imperial policy, became a supporter of the papal camp from the first.

The saying "go to Canossa" is used up to the present in most civilized languages of the world. It means to humble oneself, show repentance and remorse. The saying is connected with the name of the castle of Canossa in northern Italy, at the walls of which Henry IV stood in the winter of 1077, barefoot in a hair shirt, in order to beg forgiveness from the Pope and the removal of his excommunication. The memory of this unheard-of humiliation of the most powerful sovereign in Europe has lasted as a proverb almost a thousand years. But few of those who use it know that it was precisely the support of powerful Poland which facilitated the Pope's bringing the emperor to Canossa.

The attitude of Boleslas II (Boleslaw) the Bold in the war of investiture enabled him to regain for Poland the most important of the wasted gains of Boleslas (Boleslaw)—kingly majesty. For several months prior to Canossa, taking advantage of the weakening of the emperor's powers, he was crowned king of Poland with papal approval.

But in Poland a conspiracy of aristocrats was increasing. They could not endure the stern rule of Boleslas II. Secular and Church dignitaries, greedy for power, were especially concerned by the revival of the title of king accompanied by an increase in power. Stanislas (Stanislaw) of Szczepanow, Bishop of Cracow, was the loudest of them all in expressing his dissatisfaction. The king's pride and impetuosity hastened on the catastrophe. Angered by the public utterances of the bishop, directed against him, Boleslas II regarded them as treason and ordered that the bishop be hanged, drawn and quartered. The sentence was immediately carried out. The death of the aristocratic bishop led to a rebellion which was aided by German and Czech supporters of the emperor. The aristocrats refused to obey Boleslas and forced him to leave Poland. The throne was taken over by Prince Wladyslas (Wladyslaw) Herman, the king's incompetent brother, who was obedient to the aristocrats.

The exiled king took refuge in Hungary. Two years later he died there in mysterious circumstances. Historians believe he was murdered by persons sent from Poland. As a result of the aristocrats' conspiracy, Poland again lost its crown, the symbol of sovereignty and state unity.

And the evil specter of Popiel again ran wild in the Piast state. During the over twenty-year rule of Wladyslas Herman, the country was the scene of constant civil wars. The weak ruler yielded entirely to his palatine Sieciech, who was himself aiming to seize the throne and tried to remove from his way all the young Piast heirs. His first victim was Prince Mieszko, son of Boleslas the Bold, who returned from Hungary with his father's crown. Sieciech ordered him to be poisoned and hid the crown in the Wawel castle treasury. Afterward, with the help of Judyta, Herman's wife and sister of Emperor Henry IV, the former penitent at Canossa, Sieciech got rid of Prince Zbigniew, elder son of Wladyslas Herman, by imprisoning him in one of the German monasteries. Boleslas, Herman's younger son, happily escaped several attempts on his life.

Zbigniew fled from Germany to Bohemia, where he was supported by political opponents of Sieciech who were there in exile. Soon he set out at the head of a Polish-Czech army against Wladyslas Herman and his palatine. Chance had it that the battle between father and son took place on Lake Goplo, so closely associated with the name of Popiel. Gall the chronicler, who was perhaps a witness of the battle, states that it was very bloody. So many corpses fell into the lake, in which according to legend the bodies of the murdered uncles of Popiel were once thrown, that "every good Christian shuddered if he ate fish from that water." The father won. Zbigniew paid for his defeat by several years' imprisonment in Sieciech's castle. He was not freed until there was a rebellion of aristocrats, dissatisfied with the growing power of the palatine.

War continued for a long time in the bosom of the dynasty. First the sons fought against their father, then among themselves. The same thing was happening everywhere (perhaps fortunately for Poland): in Germany, Hungary, Bohemia and Russia. However, the Piast dynasty must have been more vital and resistant than the dynasties ruling in the neighboring states, for the latter frequently changed whereas the Piasts succeeded in outlasting the worst external and internal pressure. After every period of chaos there appeared among them a leader who in a short time remade the damages resulting from civil wars and returned unity to the country.

This time the role of savior and rebuilder was played by Wladyslas Herman's youngest son, Boleslas III, known as "Wrymouth," who ruled in the years 1102–38. We admire this king very much, since even though he did not succeed in regaining the crown for Poland, it was he who proved to be the most faithful and most fortunate continuer of the political aims of Boleslas the Bold.

After Herman's death, Boleslas and Zbigniew at first ruled Poland together, having divided it into two parts. Zbigniew leaned on the aristocracy, who were most suited by the division of the country and ruling power. However, Boleslas treated the division as a temporary state of affairs and planned to unite all the Piast territories. He was helped in this by the knights. On the model of Boleslas the Bold, Boleslas Wrymouth made alliances with the rulers of Hungary and Russia, and directed all his efforts to regain Pomerania, which as already mentioned, Poland lost at the beginning of the rule of Boleslas the Bold.

In People's Poland, which is gradually becoming a maritime state, the persistence of Boleslas Wrymouth in obtaining wide access to the Baltic is often stressed. This Piast was truly fascinated by the sea and understood its importance for Poland. One of the most eminent Polish historians recently acquainted Polish readers with a battle song of the knights of Wrymouth dating from the period of Pomeranian expeditions and written down by Gall the Anonymous. How much yearning and love for the sea can be heard in this work of the first nameless sea writer of Poland: "Salt and smelling fish sufficed our forebearers,/We are coming for fresh fish splashing in the ocean!/Our forefathers were satisfied to conquer forts,/But we are not scared by storms, nor the roar of threatening waves;/Our fathers went hunting deer,/But we shall catch treasures and monsters hidden in the ocean!"

The acquisition of Pomerania lasted nearly twenty years, with intervals. The main fortresses of these territories returned to Poland one by one: Kolobrzeg, Danzig, Szczecin. After the acquisition of Szczecin, all Pomerania was again Polish.

Because Zbigniew, supported by the aristocrats, did all he could to prevent the monarchic policy of his brother and allied himself for this purpose with the latter's enemies, Wrymouth expelled him from his territories, thus returning state unity. The strengthening on the east of the bold Polish prince disturbed the new Holy Roman emperor, Henry V. He sent an embassy to Wrymouth, demanding with the threat of war that he return to Zbigniew the territories taken from him and that he recognize the suzerainty of the emperor over Poland. To this, Boleslas made a celebrated answer, ending with the words: "If you want war, you will find it."

In 1109 the emperor's armies attacked Poland. In this war, which was forced upon Wrymouth and which by its result marked the finest page of his rule, an episode occurred often presented later in literary works: the heroic defense of Glogow.

Glogow on the central Oder, today a county town in Green Mountain (Zielona Gora) province, was at that time a fortified city. Henry V and the main forces of his armies unexpectedly crossed the Oder immediately by Glogow, after which he set about besieging the town. Despite the enormous predominance of the besiegers and the complete surprise of the defenders, all German attacks were resisted. When the emperor demanded that the citizens of Glogow surrender their city, they replied they could only do so with the permission of Prince Boleslas, who was quite far away at the time. So the emperor ordered them to send an embassy to Wrymouth. As a guarantee that the embassy would return, the town had to give hostages to the besiegers, among them the young son of the commander of the fortress. The Germans solemnly swore that the hostages would be returned no matter what reply came from Wrymouth. But when the embassy returned with a categorical order to continue defending the town, the emperor broke his promise. During the next attack, a terrible sight met the eyes of the people of Glogow: the Germans had fixed the Polish hostages, mostly young boys, to the front of their siege machines, reckoning that the defenders would not dare kill their own children. Medieval chroniclers have spared us the detailed description of the dramas of the fathers and mothers of Glogow. They restricted themselves to the dry statement that despite this inhuman behavior, the emperor failed to conquer Glogow.

Comparing events from different historical periods is often misleading. But in this case there is no way of avoiding such a comparison. Eight hundred and thirty-five years after the defense of Glogow, during the Warsaw Insurrection, an identical "military tactic" was used. Nazi tanks attacking the Insurrectionists' barricades drove crowds of Polish civilian hostages before them. At that time, the most eminent specialist of international law between the wars, Professor Zygmunt Cybichowski, died as one of these hostages. It is worth adding that in his lectures at the University of Warsaw, this scholar devoted especially large space to various international agreements (signed also by representatives of Germany) which were to assure the humanitarian treatment during wars of the civilian population, prisoners and hostages.

The turning back of the emperor at Glogow was the start of his defeats. The Germans were finally defeated on Dog Field near Wroclaw. This celebrated battlefield is now within the city of Wroclaw.

The victories and wise policies of Wrymouth again united the Piast state, rendering permanent its northern and western frontiers on the Baltic, from Szczecin through Danzig, and on the Oder and Nysa rivers. Wrymouth rebuilt Danzig from its wartime destruction and populated it with new Polish settlers. Wroclaw expanded under his rule, and the monarch often was glad to stay there.

But this wise, provident and brave Piast ended his rule with an act which wasted all the fruits of his military and political victories. The will of Boleslas Wrymouth, dated 1138, divided Poland among his four sons.

This startling act of a ruler who had striven all his life for the unification of the state has been very severely condemned by later historians. It seems, however, that there is no doubt that his motives were very human and psychologically justified.

Wrymouth lived from his youth under the pressure of misfortunes and defeats resulting from the family quarrels of the Piasts for power. He knew from tradition how much trouble Boleslas the Bold had had with his brothers, and what chaos came upon Poland as a result of the fight for the throne between the three sons of this great monarch. In childhood, he had seen the unfortunate results of disagreement between his father and uncle. Then he himself had fought for many years with his brother Zbigniew, whom he banished. Legend states that it was the result of all these horrors that a painful grimace permanently contorted the mouth of the young Boleslas. From this came his nickname: Wrymouth.

So it is not surprising that he wanted to spare his sons fraternal fighting and renewed chaos in the state whose unity and entity he had restored with such difficulty. He therefore worked out a statute of inheritance which could pass at that time as an expression of the highest political wisdom and of the best justice.

Each of his four sons inherited rule over one of Poland's historic territories. In addition, a "senior territory" was created. This largest territory, including the north and center of Poland, with its capital in Cracow, could not undergo further division and was to be ruled by the "senior," i.e., oldest in the family, assuring him at the same time superiority over all the other territories. By regulating the matter in this way, Wrymouth believed he would adequately satisfy the appetites of his successors and at the same time assure the unity of Poland, since each successive senior would be strong enough to control the general policies of the states of the remaining territorial princes.

The events of the next hundred and more years showed how illusory these calculations were.

The principal event of the period was the struggle between the Piasts for the senior territory. This started immediately after the death of Wrymouth and lasted over 150 years, until the end of the territorial state's existence. Various pretenders to the seniority did not hesitate to take advantage of foreign allies. Attacks by foreign armies (German, Russian, Czech) again started on Poland. German margraves on the frontier gained most from the weakening of Poland. In the second half of the twelfth century, they succeeded in entirely subjugating the west Slavic populations inhabiting the area between the Oder and the Spree and in creating in this area the Marches of Brandenburg, with its capital in Berlin. This new, warlike little state was in future to become a breeding place of misfortunes not only for Poland but for the whole world.

Less than fifty years after the death of Wrymouth, Poland suffered the first painful territorial loss. In 1181, Boleslas I, prince of Szczecin, seeking protection from pressure by the Brandenburg margraves, declared himself a vassal of the emperor of Germany. Western Pomerania, regained with such difficulty by Wrymouth, was detached from Poland and became permanently dependent on the German crown. The links with Danzig Pomerania also loosened, since its princes carried out their own policies without regard to the seniority passing from hand to hand in Cracow.

In the first half of the thirteenth century, the Piast states fell into even worse confusion. The first catastrophe with far-reaching effects was brought upon Poland by Konrad, prince of Mazovia and grandson of Wrymouth. The territory of this prince was always disturbed from the north by the warlike Baltic tribes of the Prussians—the same Prussians whom Boleslas the Bold had tried by means of St. Wojciech to christen and bring closer to Poland. Konrad took up the idea of his great ancestor, but in carrying it out he entrusted it to apostles who were of an entirely different type from St. Wojciech. He invited to Poland monk-knights in white cloaks with black crosses.

The Hospital Order of the Most Holy Mary of the German House in Jerusalem was formed in 1911 after the conquest of Jerusalem by the Crusade expedition of Emperor Frederick Barbarossa. At first it was a monastic order with charitable aims. Some years later it changed into a knightly order which, disappointed by its stay in the Holy Land, began offering its apostolic and military services to various European rulers whose lands bordered pagan territories. At first the Crusaders were invited to Hungary, but the king of Hungary soon realized their aggressive intentions and in 1225 he forced them to leave. It was then that Konrad of Mazovia came forward with his offer. In return for a promise to help defend the frontier against the Prussians, the prince yielded to the Teutonic Knights, as vassals, the frontier Chelmno territory. However, the role of vassals to the Polish prince did not suit the Order. By devious machinations they obtained from the emperor and the Pope a confirmation of the "gift" of the Chelmno territory, and also Prussia, though the latter was not yet acquired. After carrying out the legal formalities, the Knights transferred their energy to apostolic functions and occupied themselves with converting the Prussians to Christianity. They applied methods different from those of St. Wojciech. Instead of the cross, they used the sword. They stamped out pagans along with paganism.

In this manner a new German state began forming at high speed on the northern edges of Mazovia and on the Baltic. The main enemies hitherto of the Piasts—the emperors of the Holy Roman Empire (Germany)—could peacefully preoccupy themselves with the western problems of their extensive empire. Reliable guards were left on the Polish frontiers—the Marches of Brandenburg and the state of the Teutonic Knights. The two new German states were not interested in the west, all their policy being subordinate to one main idea, viz. movement east (*Drang nach Osten*). This was to affect Poland's future catastrophically.

Another historical catastrophe occurred in Silesia. At this time, when Konrad of Mazovia was bringing about the emergence of the Crusaders' state in the north of Poland, the thought was ripening in the south of the rebirth of a united Polish kingdom. It was represented by two eminent Piasts who lived in Wroclaw: Henryk I the Bearded, and then his son Henryk II the Pious. Henryk the Bearded succeeded in bringing under his rule inherited Silesia with Poznan and Gniezno. Henryk the Pious took over all his father's inheritance and continued his plans of unification, aiming to be crowned king of all Poland. But when it seemed that he had almost fulfilled this aim, an unexpected cataclysm visited the southern part of the country. The first Tartar invasion occurred, led by the famous Subutaj, one of the most celebrated leaders of Genghis Khan. The enemy was powerful, well trained in the trade of war and used new means of war: gunpowder, also primitive flamethrowers and poison gases (or so it would appear from descriptions of contemporary chroniclers). At the time of the invasion of Poland, the empire created by Genghis Khan occupied the area from the river Yangtze in China to the Dnieper and Don. So far, no one had been able to resist the Tartar cavalry fighting force. The heavily armed Silesian, Little Polish and Great Polish knights, helped by peasants and miners from Silesia and also by two units of monastic knights, the Crusaders and Templars, could not resist them either.

On April 9, 1241, in the battle of Silesian Legnica, the Polish Army, led personally by Henryk the Pious, was terribly defeated. The would-be king of Poland perished, and his head was impaled, while the armies underwent complete destruction.

With this event, plans for unifying the state and regaining the crown were laid aside for a long time. The times of Popiel had returned with a vengeance. The principle of seniority laid down by Wrymouth disappeared entirely. Various territories gradually underwent increasing subdivision. Poland was changed into a loose association of small states, the rulers of which carried on a permanent battle with each other. At odds, the Piasts committed violent acts against one another, locked up, maimed and even killed one another. Meanwhile, the strength of the external enemies of the divided state continued to grow. The margraves of Brandenburg purchased the Lubusk territory on the Oder from one of the Piasts and soon afterward subjected western Pomerania, with Szczecin and Kolobrzeg, to their rule. Matters were just as bad in the north. In a few decades, the Crusaders defeated all Prussia and took eastern Pomerania, having previously cut down the Polish population of Danzig. It is worth noting that a Polish prince summoned the Crusaders to Danzig to defend the town against the Brandenburgs. The Lithuanians and Tartars attacked Poland from the east. The Germanized kings of Bohemia interfered in the business of the Piasts on the south, claiming the right to the Polish crown for themselves for various reasons. The Czech pressure was primarily on Silesia, which had dissolved into individual small states after the death of Henryk the Pious. The Silesian Piasts, still at odds with each other, yielded especially easily to external influences and quickly became Germanized or Czechs.

From time to time, however, some energetic and politically gifted prince emerged from the territorial chaos and gathered several territories under his rule, attempting to bring order to the entire country. One such was Przemyslas II of Greater Poland, who did not, to be sure, conclude his unification task, but succeeded in being crowned in 1295, with the Pope's approval, as king of all Poland with the former crown of Boleslas the Bold. But he did not reign long. Seven months later, when the king was fast asleep after a carnival, the margraves of Brandenburg attacked and killed him in a cruel manner.

After the death of Przemyslas II, a violent struggle broke out between his successors. A foreign monarch, Waclaw II, the king of Bohemia, supported by the Holy Roman emperor Albrecht Hapsburg, came out victorious. He attacked at the head of strong Czech-German armies and was crowned king of Poland in Gniezno in 1300. This coronation was not regarded as legal, as papal permission was not obtained, but no one could take his actual authority from Waclaw II. The five-year rule of this monarch, forced on Poland by the German emperor, was unusually damaging to Poland, but it was fortunately the last victory of the sinister Popiel line. Again a Piast rebuilder appeared on the scene—Wladyslas, prince of Leczyca and Kujavia.

The longtime rival and later heir to King Waclaw II was a man of great intelligence and character, but he was so small that his contemporaries called him "the Short."

Wladyslas the Short had an unusually hard life. He spent over forty years in continual battles with external and internal enemies. Exiled from Poland by Waclaw II, he returned secretly and for a long time had to hide from the German officials of the king. In Ojcow near Cracow, one of the most beautiful locations in Poland, to this day are shown labyrinths or grottoes in which the "short king" is supposed to have hidden, defended by his peasant partisans.

Not until 1320 did Wladyslas the Short, by now an old man, succeed in being crowned the king of all Poland, thus terminating the period of territorial division. The solemn coronation took place in the Wawel and from that time Cracow became the official capital of the Polish kingdom. Poland emerged from the territorial period with the loss of the Chelmno territory, western and eastern Pomerania and the Lubusk territory. Soon Silesia also broke away.

In time, the Jagiellonians regained some of these territories, but most of them did not return to Poland until 1945.

The rule of Wladyslas the Short started a long period of power and eminence for the Polish state. The son of this ruler was Kazimierz the Great, "king of the peasants." In this manner the circle closed. For after all it was from the tomb of Wladyslas the Short's son that we started our tour around the Wawel mausoleum, leading our readers into the second part of the history of Poland, her highest achievement and deepest decline.

You already know that at the end of the eighteenth century, the Polish state ceased to exist and its territories were divided among the three neighboring powers: the Russian Empire, the Holy Roman Empire (Germany) (after the dissolution by Napoleon of the Reich of German states, the Hapsburgs on the imperial throne started calling themselves emperors of Austria) and the kingdom of Prussia (the kings of Prussia took the title of German emperors after 1871).

Historians consider that the main cause of the catastrophe of the partitions was Prussia. Russia and Austria were more concerned with subjugating the Polish state politically than with partitioning and liquidating it. But overpopulated Prussia, imbued with a militaristic spirit and faithful to its main political aim of *Drang nach Osten,* aimed constantly at expanding its "living space" by means of further territorial acquisitions in the east. This is why the plan for partitioning Poland came from Berlin. This is not merely a hypothesis of historians. It is known that after the first partition, Prince Henry of Prussia, the brother of the rapacious king of Prussia, Frederick II, demanded a statement on paper from Empress Catherine of Russia that it was he who was the real author of the partitioning idea. It is worth remembering that the kingdom of Prussia arose as a result of the union of Brandenburg with the territory of the Prussian Crusaders, these two German states having arisen from the mistakes and weaknesses of the Polish territorial princes. So the statement may be risked that the roots of the partitions of Poland reach back to the period of the territorial divisions.

Poland was enslaved for 120 years. Until the outbreak of the First World War in 1914, a Pole wishing to visit the three historical capitals of his own country—Poznan, Cracow and Warsaw—had to cross at least two frontiers. Poznan was divided from Cracow by the German-Austrian frontier, Cracow from Warsaw by the Austro-Russian frontier, and Warsaw from Poznan by the Russian-German frontier.

Despite these frontiers dividing Poland into three parts, despite the political terrorism and nationality pressure applied in all the zones, despite the driving out of the Polish language from schools and offices, the rapacious powers did not succeed in the course of 120 years in damaging the biological, historical and cultural unity of the Polish people, or in weakening their national awareness. A secret resistance movement existed all these years in the three zones. Every now and then an armed insurrection burst out in one or other of these zones, causing an immediate echo in the other zones. To orientate our readers in the strength of the independence movement, it is worth listing the dates and locations of outbreaks of various national and liberational insurrections: 1794, Kosciuszko's insurrection in Cracow; 1806, an insurrection in Greater Poland; 1831, the November insurrection in Warsaw; 1846, the insurrection in Cracow; 1848, insurrection in Greater Poland; 1863, the January insurrection in Warsaw. Some of these insurrections extended throughout the country. Kosciuszko's insurrection and the January insurrection became regular wars, lasting for months. The 1806 Greater Poland insurrection, raised after the entry of French troops, forced the emperor Napoleon to create a miniature Polish state called the Duchy of Warsaw, which existed throughout all the Napoleonic campaigns and lasted another fifteen years as an autonomous Polish kingdom under the rule of the Russian tsars.

After the defeat of the January insurrection, the desperate partisan struggles of which lasted over eighteen months in the forests and which brought on particularly bloody and destructive retaliation from the partitioning powers, no further attempts at insurrection were undertaken. A new social class, the proletariat, gradually began to take the main initiative in the fight for independence. The national liberation movement took on at the same time characteristics of a revolutionary social movement. The socialist parties leading it tried to make their strategy agree with that of the revolutionary movements throughout Europe, especially in the partitioning states. The shape of the struggle with the partitioning states changed. Instead of insurrections, workers' demonstrations, political strikes

Grave of Tadeusz Kosciuszko. Cracow

Festival on the stage of the amphitheater on top of St. Ahn mountain

in industry and schools against the Russification and Germanization of teaching broke out from the second half of the nineteenth century. Bomb attacks were made on especially hated partitioning governor-generals and police chiefs.

In both the first and second phase of the fighting for independence, every urge toward freedom by Poles was brutally suppressed by the partitioning governments. After every insurrection and revolutionary disturbance, thousands of patriots had to leave Poland to avoid police repressions. Political emigration became a mass phenomenon in Poland much earlier than emigration for work. Polish political emigrees were scattered throughout the whole world. Unable to fight for the freedom of their own homeland, they more than once went down in history fighting for the liberty of other nations. Tadeusz Kosciuszko and Kazimierz Pulaski fought for the independence of the United States. Joseph (Jozef) Bem, who took part in the January insurrection, led a Hungarian army in 1848 in a war of liberation against Austria and Russia. In the same year, the great Polish poet Adam Mickiewicz organized a Slavic legion in Rome to help the Italian revolutionaries in their fight with Austria. In 1871, two organizers of the January insurrection, Jarowslaw Dabrowski and Valery Wroblewski, led the defense of Paris, besieged by the Prussians. These are only the most important and best-known names. But it may be boldly stated that during Poland's 120 years of enslavement, there was not a single liberation war or revolution throughout the world in which Polish political emigrees did not take part. The Polish emigration left many traces in the history of other countries. Suffice it to say that on the map of the United States there are over ten townships named Warsaw, not to mention others named Kosciuszko or Pulaski.

For Poles, the most beautiful and dearest inheritance from the emigration is the present national anthem of the Polish state. Its tune is known to all those taking part or watching great international sporting events. It resounds from loudspeakers whenever a Polish athlete wins an event, and this happens quite often. A foreigner hearing it for the first time cannot help being surprised. It is hard for him to believe that this lively melody, almost a dance tune in the rhythm of a mazurka (a lively Polish folk dance; Chopin's mazurkas are particularly well known), can be a national anthem. He would be still more surprised if he knew that the Polish national anthem begins with the words: "Poland has not yet perished as long as we are still alive." The statement contained in these words may seem naïve and even boastful, but only to those people who do not know the origins of the anthem and its later fate.

The Polish national anthem, commonly called "Dabrowski's Mazurka," arose in Italy in 1797, i.e., three years after the defeat of Kosciuszko's insurrection. The defeat forced thousands of soldiers and patriotic civilians to leave their country. Most of these enforced exiles gathered in revolutionary France, which was at the time carrying on a war with one of the partitioners of Poland, the emperor of Austria. The main front of this war was in Italy, where General Bonaparte, later the emperor Napoleon, was just gaining his first great victories over the Austrians. Former leaders of the insurrection in France gained permission from the French government to form Polish legions alongside Bonaparte's army. From this time, Polish volunteers began proceeding to Italy, believing that Napoleon's victories would make it possible for them to regain their free homeland. General Jan Henryk Dabrowski (not to be confused with Jarowslaw Dabrowski, who defended Paris from the Germans in later years), one of Kosciuszko's most eminent leaders, was the organizer and leader of the Polish legions in Italy.

As an experienced leader, General Dabrowski knew that nothing raises a soldier's spirits better than a good song. So he suggested to his friend, the writer Joseph (Jozef) Wybicki, a former member of the insurrection government, that he write a song for the legions. The patriotic writer succeeded very well in his task. To the tune of a folk mazurka, he expressed all the great yearning of Polish exiles for their homeland and all their faith in ultimate victory. The main idea of the song is that although the name of Poland be erased from all the maps of the world, although its territories were split up between the partitioning powers, Poland exists and will continue to exist as long as there are Polish patriots.

This is precisely the idea which Wybicki expressed in the words "Poland has not yet perished as long as we are still alive."

"Dabrowski's Mazurka" accompanied Polish soldiers through all the years of the Napoleonic campaign. And although Napoleon did not fulfill the hopes placed in him by the Poles, the legion hymn outlived his fall and took on ever more strength and meaning. It became a nationwide song of hope and belief in ultimate victory. For over a century, the words "Poland has not yet perished" were a slogan uniting the Poles of the three zones.

It was with this song on their lips that Warsaw cadets drove the Grand Duke Constanty, the tsar's governor-general, from the capital in November 1830. During the "Spring of the Peoples" in 1848 this song was to be heard on the barricades of Vienna, Berlin, Paris and Rome. In the winter of 1863, partisans of the January insurrection in the forests took heart with the song. It was sung during workers' revolutionary demonstrations in the streets of Warsaw and Lodz in 1905–7 and during the school strikes in Greater Poland and in the Russian zone.

When Poland regained independence in 1918, it was demanded that the song, which had done service in the fights for freedom, become the official national anthem, but for certain complicated reasons, which cannot be gone into here, it was not awarded that honor until 1926. From that time, the lively "Dabrowski's Mazurka" has been the solemn symbol of the Polish state.

During World War II, the hymn lost its venerable character of a national monument, since its former meaning came to life under the influence of current events of the war; it again became a soldiers' song of yearning and hope. The Poles had every right to boast that apart from themselves no other nation in the world had a national anthem that harmonized so well with the fate of the nation. "Dabrowski's Mazurka" resounded in all parts of the world. It was hummed in low tones at conspiratorial meetings in occupied Polish towns and at the campfires of partisans in the forests. Its lively tune was heard wherever Polish soldiers were fighting, at Narvik in Norway, Tobruk in Africa, Lenino in the Soviet Union and Monte Cassino in Italy. Polish airmen sang it before taking off on air raids from French and Scottish airfields. And Polish sailors fighting in northern and southern seas sang it. It resounded triumphantly at the liberation of every Polish town. Then the First Army took it as far as Berlin.

In the last weeks of the Second World War, Poles listening to this state anthem experienced strange and startling feelings in many localities in Poland. It seemed to them that the lively tune of the mazurka was echoed by the many-voiced sound of distant centuries of history. They could clearly hear the heavy tread of Boleslas the Bold's fighting men. And a solemn song of the troops of Boleslas Wrymouth. And the groans of the defenders of Glogow. And the cries of the Polish garrison in Danzig murdered by the Crusader monk-knights. And the mingled noise of the nocturnal attack of the Brandenburg murderers on sleeping King Przemyslas.

This occurred when the Polish national anthem was played for the first time on the ruins of Danzig and Kolobrzeg, on the ruins of Szczecin and Wroclaw.

It is difficult to believe that only twenty-five years have passed since the Potsdam conference of the three great powers, the Soviet Union, the United States and Great Britain, at which the western frontier of the Polish state was laid down along the Oder and Nysa rivers, which enabled Poland to return to the territories of the former Piast state.

On April 1, 1945, the ruins of Danzig were still breathing fire and smoke, when the first Polish provincial governor, the engineer Okecki, without a tie and wearing shabby Warsaw clothes, took the city of Danzig under the rule of the Republic. How many times in the course of its history had Danzig

The Grunwald obelisk

waited longingly for this ceremony. After the famous massacre of the Crusader Knights at Grunwald in 1410, uncounted crowds of the townspeople of Crusader Danzig enthusiastically greeted the representative of King Wladyslas Jagiello, the Castellan Janusz of Tuliszkow. But the Polish victory was not taken advantage of, and the Crusaders took a bloody revenge on the citizens of Danzig for their premature rejoicing. An enormous fine was levied on the city. When the citizens refused to pay, the leader of the Crusaders asked representatives of the city to bargain. Two burgomasters, Konrad Leczkow and Arnold Hecht, went to the castle with a lawyer Bartholomew (Bartlomiej) Gross. A week later, the Crusaders handed over their murdered bodies to the citizens.

During the almost thousand years since Mieszko I founded the city, Danzig belonged to the Crusaders for 146 years, to the German Reich for 125 years, and for 20 years held the status of a free city. For the remaining 700 years Danzig was ruled by Polish kings and princes.

The population of the city had an international character for a very long time, probably since the territorial period. Germans, Dutch, Poles, French and Italians lived here. The following celebrated individuals originated from Danzig: Jan Dantyszek, one of the greatest Polish humanists and secretary to King Zygmunt the Old: Jan Heweliusz, the greatest Polish astronomer after Copernicus; Daniel Fahrenheit, the German-Dutch physicist who invented the first mercury thermometer; Jan Forster, who took part in James Cook's expedition round the world and later became a professor at a Polish university; Daniel Chodowiecki, a fine Polish-French painter, to whose drawings we owe a fine survey of Danzig townsfolk in the eighteenth century; and finally Arthur Schopenhauer, one of the greatest German philosophers. All of them considered themselves to the end of their lives, no matter where they lived, as people of Danzig. Even Schopenhauer, the glory of German science and literature, protested when he was called a German.

Danzig was a proud and bold city which strongly defended its rights, not only against the Crusaders and Germans but also against Polish kings. But it was firmly and truly attached to Poland. It bore witness to this many times in the worst moments. In the seventeenth century, during the Swedish wars under the Vasa dynasty, when the whole country was flooded with a deluge of foreign armies and the state had in fact ceased to exist, Danzig, despite much persuasion from the king of Sweden, remained the only town which stayed unshaken on the side of the king of Poland. After the first partition, only the desperate resistance of Danzig caused it not to be seized by the king of Prussia. Two years later, after the second partition, the people of Danzig broke down the gate of the arsenal, armed themselves and greeted Prussian units entering the town with fire from the ramparts. Fine proofs of patriotism and ingenuity were given by the people of Danzig during the January insurrection of 1863, smuggling arms to the insurrectionists in pianofortes which had rifles, guns and swords in the place of strings. The gilded statue of King Zygmunt Augustus, last of the Jagiellos, which adorns the top of the town hall, is a lasting monument to the emotional attitude of Danzig to Poland (it was recently rebuilt after the wartime destruction). Chauvinistic Nazi propaganda concealed it under the name "the golden boy" when describing it in guidebooks. Nor was the Latin inscription on the statue mentioned, which reads: *Aurea Sarmatiae redeant sic tempora nostrae* (Oh, that our golden Polish times might return).

The inscription was not servile insincerity, but had full historical justification. Danzig flourished most splendidly under the rule of Poland, and faded under the rule of the Crusaders or Prussia. This was understandable. The Polish gentry were not much interested in the sea, but traded widely. All the country's exports and imports came through Danzig, filling the chests of Danzig merchants, shippers and bankers with gold.

During the last months of World War I, when the news reached Danzig that President Wilson of the United States had read the famous Fourteen Points program on January 9, 1918, and declared in Point 13 that Poland would remain within her ethnic borders with access to the sea, the local Poles immediately believed that Danzig would be Polish. They made every effort to prevent the Germans from removing machinery and other property away from the city.

Unfortunately, matters turned out differently. At the Versailles peace conference on June 28, it was decided that Danzig and its region would be a "free city." As well as Danzig, other former Piast territories were excluded from the Second Republic, e.g., western Pomerania and the larger part of Silesia. Masuria, i.e., the southern part of the former Crusader territory in Prussia, inhabited mainly by Polish settlers and clearly belonging to Poland, was also outside Polish frontiers. To be sure, plebiscites were held in some of these territories under the control of international commissions, and the population of upper Silesia three times organized desperate insurrections to join the entire region with Poland, but this did not help much, since the appropriate support from the government was lacking at the decisive moment, as it was preoccupied at the time with the Polish-Soviet war proceeding in the east. (After this war, the eastern frontier of the Second Republic included part of the areas of the former Jagiellonian state, located east of the river Bug with seven million Lithuanians, White Russians and Ukrainians. After World War II, as a result of resolutions of the three great powers taken at Yalta in the Crimea, these territories were incorporated in the three Soviet republics of Lithuania, Belorussia and the Ukraine. Poles who lived in these territories were repatriated to the Polish People's Republic.)

As a result, Poland gained access to the Baltic only along a narrow strip of the former Danzig area of Pomerania, out of which territory was also sliced for the new miniature state called the Free City of Danzig. This narrow neck of the Second Republic, stretching to the sea (soon the name Polish Corridor was used for it in the newspapers of the whole world), was enclosed by the claws of two parts of the German state, formerly Prussia and western Pomerania.

If the statesmen at Versailles who created these frontiers of Poland thought they were creating something permanent, then they were at least as credulous and shortsighted as Boleslas Wrymouth when he signed his will. Anyone with a knowledge of history and the methods employed by German militarism could have foreseen without difficulty that the Polish Corridor would become a pretext for Germany to unleash a new war.

The little state of the Free City of Danzig occupied an area of some 1,200 square miles, had about 350,000 inhabitants and was governed by a senate. Poland obtained a number of privileges in the Free City: she conducted the foreign policy of Danzig, controlled the railroad, took part in regulating the port and waterways, retained her own mail service. But these privileges were systematically undermined by the senate. During less than twenty years of relations between Danzig and Poland, seventy important conflicts occurred. These conflicts had to be solved by the High Commissioner, who looked after the interests of the Free City in the League of Nations (which corresponded at that time to the present-day United Nations).

In 1930, Hitler's representative Albert Forster arrived in Danzig, where he organized the Nazi Party. Militant chauvinism began increasing in the territory of the Free City. This was immediately reflected in the attitude toward local Poles. A year after the arrival of Forster, one of the most active Polish supporters was murdered in front of the Danzig office of the Polish state railroads. Nazi gangs attacked Polish schools and hit people who spoke Polish in the street.

Meanwhile, in Poland, on which Versailles had bestowed

A shipyard at the port of Gdynia

such narrow access to the Baltic, interest in the sea and an understanding of its importance for the country had grown from the first moment of independence. Love for the sea appeared in works of art and propaganda. A concrete expression of this new passion for the Poles was the largest economic investment of the years between the wars, viz. the building of the port of Gdynia, not far from Danzig. Poland's first seaport became the apple of the nation's eye and a quite dangerous rival of Danzig. Gdynia facilitated the training of modest but (as the later war was to show) good cadres of the Polish commercial and military navy.

Shortly before the war, during the period of the tragic flirtation between the political directorship of the Second Republic and the Nazi Reich, a German battleship paid a "courtesy visit" to Gdynia. This visit had a very disagreeable effect on the inhabitants of Gdynia. The young cadets of the *Kriegsmarine*, dressed in white parade shirts, with long ribbons on their caps, did not hide their contempt for the small Polish units anchored in the military port. In the streets of the city they behaved as though they were at home. Their arrogant laughter was hard for the Poles to endure.

The Second World War started in Danzig. Early in the morning of September 1, 1939, the battleship *Schleswig-Holstein* started firing on Westerplatte, a Polish military storehouse located in the port of Gdynia. At the same time, units of uniformed Nazis, police and troops attacked the building of the Polish mail. A few post officials and mail carriers defended themselves for fourteen hours. They surrendered only after the Germans brought artillery and flamethrowers and set fire to the building. Six post-office workers fell in the battle, six died in the hospital of wounds, while thirty-nine were immediately shot by sentence of a field court. Those officials and mail carriers who were not in the building that day were immediately arrested and sent to concentration camps. They all perished.

The staff of Westerplatte, on a small peninsula at the mouth of the Vistula, amounted to 182 soldiers and civilian workers. Westerplatte, bombed ceaselessly from land, air and water, defended itself for seven days. Lack of ammunition and medicine for the wounded forced the defenders to surrender.

Much was written about these two episodes of the defense of Poland's rights to the sea in the press of the whole world. Two startling movies were made in Poland recently, based on these events. The name Westerplatte has remained a monumental word for us until the present.

After the joining of Danzig to the Third Reich, Albert Forster, appointed gauleiter, bloodily attacked Poles. He condemned Polish teachers and Boy Scout activists with special hatred. Under Forster's rule, over 65,000 people died in the concentration camp at Stutthof (now Sztutowo) which "served" the Danzig area.

In the second half of January 1945, the Soviet offensive, in which Polish units also took part, started approaching the Baltic. Danzig found itself in the range of harassing air raids and artillery fire. Forster insisted on defending the city. Workers were not allowed to leave factories despite air raids. The remainder of the population spent whole days in shelters. When the generals Specht and Weiss regarded the defense of Danzig as impossible and decided to surrender the town, Forster—after consulting Hitler's headquarters—ordered them arrested and had them sent by a special airplane to Berlin for execution. On March 22, Soviet troops reached the Baltic in the area of the famous resort Sopot in the neighborhood of Danzig. Two days later, leaflets thrown from airplanes urged the town to surrender: "Your resistance is vain and will only lead to the destruction of you and hundreds of thousands of women, children and old people . . ." But Forster did not yield, supported by a telegram from the Führer's headquarters: "Every square meter of the Danzig-Gdynia region must be firmly defended."

The Westerplatte monument, where World War II began

In this manner one of the most beautiful towns in Europe was condemned to destruction (Schopenhauer called its architecture "stone music").

At this point, some readers may have doubts whether it is permissible in one and the same book to praise the defense of Warsaw and then condemn that of Danzig. After all, the defense was hopeless in both cases and caused equally heavy losses. But it was not the same. Warsaw, attacked treacherously by the enemy, defended itself by the will of its entire population. The foundations of that defense were love for their own city and the wish to protest against foreign domination. But Danzig was defended under Nazi terror. The resistance of this defense did not spring from noble feelings but cowardly fear. Gauleiter Forster was afraid to surrender, because he was guilty of so many crimes that he could not hope for forgiveness from the victors. A conscientious chronicler of those times stated on the basis of archival documents what a cowardly individual Hitler's governor-general was. At the same moment when all the architectural treasures of Danzig and tens of thousands of human beings were condemned to destruction, Gauleiter Forster was organizing the removal of his furniture to the Reich in a safe shelter on Hel Peninsula.

On March 28, 1945, soldiers of the Polish tank brigade named after the heroes of Westerplatte struck a red and white flag on the Danzig "Arus Court," which at one time housed Polish monarchs. Fighting lasted two more days in the city. A war correspondent present at the capture of Danzig wrote: "The huge city is burning, set on fire by the shells of German ships and German flares. Many-storied buildings are falling with a crash to the ground. The city is drowning in black smoke, and it is difficult to breathe the heated air. Fighting continues in the streets."

About a year after these events, a tall thin man in gray prison clothes sat in the dock in a temporary courtroom in a suburb of Danzig. A lawyer sitting beside him translated into German the successive points of the act of accusation, read out by the judge. Every now and then the accused wiped the sweat from his forehead with a handkerchief, after which he looked fearfully around the hall; on catching anyone's eye, he smiled humbly and apologetically. The smile of Albert Forster was the opposite of the arrogant smiles of the young German sailors who visited Gdynia before the war. But it was still more intolerable.

At the time when the former Nazi gauleiter was answering for his crimes in the Danzig court, a historic process of re-Polonization, resettlement and rebuilding was being carried out throughout the Regained Territories (such was the official name at the time) on the Baltic, Oder and Nysa. Today, twenty-five years later, these three words—re-Polonization, resettlement and rebuilding—are lightly and easily said. But their real weight, the enormity and complexity of the problems contained in them can only be appreciated by those who have not yet forgotten those times.

Those times! Dozens of miles of uninhabited space, burned out by war. On walls damaged by shells, large black inscriptions, Rache! (Revenge), left by the retreating Nazis. Factories and mines devastated and looted of their equipment. The entry to ports blocked by the wrecks of sunken boats and ships. Railroads without rails. Houses without doors, windows often without roofs. The ruins of Danzig, Kolobrzeg, Szczecin, Wroclaw, Legnica, terrifying with the Gothic letters of German notices. Unlike the Warsaw ruins, familiar objects and the still warm traces of presence a few months earlier were not to be found there. Proof of ownership had to be documented by the worn-out Latin inscriptions on the Piast monuments and Polish names on nineteenth-century epitaphs in old cemeteries.

Transports of German population traveled west every day. Transports of repatriated people from the other side of the

Bug arrived every day, to whose lot had fallen the closing of accounts from the times of the Piasts and Jagiellos. Nights were restless in the villages of western Pomerania and Masuria; the first settlers had to barricade themselves in their homes like forts for fear of attacks by robbers or diversionists from the Nazi Wehrwolf (a Nazi organization which operated during the first postwar years in Masuria and Pomerania). The lack of light, water, the most necessary furniture and equipment, and means of communication were painfully felt. There was a lot of muddle and many unjust regulations. The first neighborly contacts between the new arrivals from other areas of Poland with the local population, who spoke Polish somewhat differently but legitimized themselves by the fact that they had not let their Polishness be rooted out for a hundred years, were made with enormous resistance. And later, when people began to get used to the new landscapes, houses and neighbors, anonymous letters with threats started arriving from the other side of the Laba: "Don't think it is yours . . . We shall return!"

Those were exceedingly difficult times. Sometimes even strong people after a stay of some months in the "Wild West" (the phrase was borrowed from American movies) gave up and came to the conclusion that a century would be necessary to settle these territories and unite them entirely with the old country.

And yet it happened long before a quarter of a century passed. Already for several years it has become an obvious fact to all that no one in the world, even the most determined enemy of Poland, dares question it.

The amount of work put into settling, restoring and taking over these territories can be imagined only by definite examples, but how to show these examples in the most convincing manner? If this little book were a tourist guide we would lead our readers in turn around all the most important towns of the Western and Northern Territories. We would start from Wroclaw, the former capital of the two Henryks of Silesia, a town pulsating with life and energy, a great industrial center and the third (after Warsaw and Cracow) scientific and artistic center of Poland, a town whose scholars and artists already have worldwide renown, in which railroad trucks, electronic machines and movies are produced, in which several national scholarly periodicals are published and where about 30,000 students are being educated.

Then we would show Opole, crowded with colorful, singing young people during the annual song festival, and all the Opole region, where nearly a million Poles survived many centuries of Germanization. And Zielona Gora, with its colorful historic processions on the day of the vine gathering. And pretty wooded Szczecin with its imposing castle of the Pomeranian princes, a town of shipyards and sailors, students and archaeologists. And the huge complex of the three cities Gdynia, Sopot and Danzig, linked together in a very strangely harmonious manner: great shipbuilding industry, seaports, fishing centers, the most frequented Baltic bathing resorts, wonderful monuments of old architecture, brokers' offices and one of the best assemblies in the country of artists and sculptors.

But this little book is not a tourist guide, so we cannot permit ourselves the detailed description of all these cities or of many other localities worth showing. Instead, we will restrict ourselves to quoting some information and figures which will characterize Polish achievements on the Baltic, Oder and Nysa.

To begin with, almost all the larger cities in these territories were occupied by Poland as uninhabited ruins and sites. In any case this was how Wroclaw, Szczecin and Danzig looked, as the Nazis converted them in the last weeks of the war into fortresses, defended with unparalleled stubbornness. Wroclaw,

A beach on the Baltic Sea

evacuated of civilians, was defending itself even after the fall of Berlin, as a result of which it became one of the largest and most terrible battlefields of World War II.

It is precisely from the example of Wroclaw that we can understand best what an indescribably difficult task it was to settle and Polonize the Western Territories. The population of this great city started from the very beginning—from absolute zero. They consisted of newcomers from all parts of the country and also from abroad: prisoners returning from Nazi concentration and prisoner-of-war camps, repatriates from the other side of the river Bug, peasant colonists, seekers of adventures and people escaping from their previous lives. Only a small proportion of this new population came from large cities. Over 40 per cent had lived previously in small townships, and another 40 per cent came straight from the countryside. In the course of not quite twenty-five years, this indescribable human mixture, extremely varied as regards geographical and social origin and habits, was transformed into a compact urban community. The speedup of this process was most helped by young people, for whom the differences dividing their elders were no longer so important. Now almost half the population of Wroclaw were born in the city. Young people give the city its tone and shape its cultural and social aspects and its habits. The other towns and localities of the Regained Territories had a population situation like that of Wroclaw. This was less difficult only in the Opole region and in Masuria, where compact groups of the local Polish population survived. But today, the local patriotism of the inhabitants of Wroclaw, Szczecin, Danzig, Olsztyn and Zielona Gora can boldly rival the local patriotism of the people of Warsaw, Cracow or Poznan.

Figures concerning employment in industry speak best of the degree of cultivation of these territories. In 1945, the Poles took over former German industry in a state of complete destruction. People who remember those times state that there

was not a single industrial establishment in Wroclaw, Danzig
or Szczecin which could be started without large investments.
Today around a million people are employed in the industries of the Western and Northern Territories, which is more
than in all Poland's industry before the war.

Poland's access to the 500-kilometer Baltic coast has made
it a maritime country. Before the war, Poland did not have its
own shipyards. Today the three great Baltic ports of Gdynia,
Danzig and Szczecin are at the same time large shipbuilding
centers. The Polish shipbuilding industry already occupies a
high place in world production. People who were reaping corn
in 1949 on the site of Nowa Huta, now on vacation on the
Baltic, have the opportunity of seeing great merchant ships
built in Polish shipyards in the ports of Gdynia and Danzig, on
which full factory equipment also entirely produced in Poland
is being exported to distant lands. Such sights allow them to
evaluate to the full the development of the industrialization of
the country from the historical reaping at Wanda's Mound.

The degree to which the Western and Northern Territories
have grown into the rest of Poland, and at the same time the
entire absurdity of the prewar frontiers on west and north, can
best be felt in two Polish cities: Gdynia and Katowice. For a
young student of Gdynia, who travels by bus to the beach at
Sopot or to the movies in Danzig, and is to start studying in
the fall at the polytechnical college in Szczecin, the fact that
these cities were separated by state frontiers is just as hard to
realize as the fact that before World War I, Warsaw, Poznan
and Cracow were separated in a similar way.

Or Katowice. This city is the main center of the Upper
Silesian industrial region, a capital of miners whose traditional
black clothes and round cap with black or white plumes
awaken the deepest respect all over Poland, far and wide.
Every Pole knows what a treasure coal is for Poland and what
a role the labor of the Silesian coal miners played in the re-

building of Warsaw and other cities, and in the development of Polish industry. Katowice was the capital of Upper Silesia before the war too, and a large center of industry and mining. But as a result of the division of Silesia into two parts it became a frontier city, which was inexpressibly dangerous and rendered its further development impossible. The German part of Upper Silesia was not properly developed economically, since the Germans treated it only as supplementary to the Ruhr basin. After the shift of the frontiers to the Oder and Nysa, the situation underwent a fundamental change. The return to Poland of Gliwice and Bytom, which today create with Katowice an organic economic entity, the regaining of the agricultural support of the Opole region and the link with the Oder give to the city and the entire industrial center enormous opportunities of development. Today Katowice is already the most modern and most urbanized city in Poland. Its plans for the future drive our economic journalists crazy.

The territories returned to Poland in 1945 were at first named the Regained Territories, and later—when they had reached a sufficient degree of Polonization—they were renamed the Western and Northern Territories. This has remained so to the present. Recently, however, this separate naming has been causing more and more objections. People write that the constant stressing that Wroclaw, Szczecin, Zielona Gora, Koszalin, Olsztyn and other cities are located in the Western or Northern Territories is as absurd as writing that Warsaw is located in the center of the country, and Cracow in the south. The territories on the Baltic, Oder and Nysa are quite simply Polish and require no other epithets.

All this allows us to understand what an important role the problems of the Oder-Nysa frontier play in Polish life. This frontier is in fact recognized throughout the world. But as no peace treaty has yet been made with Germany, many states continually prohibit its recognition in an official manner. This is an unpleasant situation for the Poles, since it gives the opportunity for revisionist outbursts by various heirs of Nazism.

An "anti-German complex" is often attributed to Poles. Indeed, the experiences of the last war might bring certain complexes upon nervous people. But complexes are a symptom of sickness. A normal, honest Polish patriot, the citizen of a country in which for six years Poles were tortured and murdered only because they were Poles, must admit that the evaluation of people according to their nationality is criminal stupidity. One yardstick for evaluation of a Polish patriot's attitude to the Germans and the two German states can be his attitude to the Oder-Nysa frontier. For this attitude is closely associated with his attitude to the Crusader-Prussian-Nazi idea of *Drang nach Osten*, the results of which the Poles know as well from history as from their own experiences.

The millennium of the Polish state was celebrated by a beautiful and useful social act: with the money collected from the contributions of citizens, a thousand memorial schools were built. These schools are known colloquially as "thousanders," and can easily be distinguished, since they are all alike: large, bright, of modern design. They are to be found in various parts of the country: near famous historical battlefields, in locations of national martyrdom, in cities and villages associated with the memory of great events.

One of the "thousanders" can be seen from the windows of the present writer. When he wondered whether he had put down everything he had to say, the bell for lessons rang in the school opposite and the children ran in to class. The writer's typewriter began to tap out fervent thoughts and wishes: that these schools remain permanent memorials of the Polish millennium, not only in a material sense, but also spiritually; that the finest and most progressive traditions of our history be preserved in them; that love be taught in them for the uniting,

Millennium memorial school

provident Piast line, and hatred for the destructive, criminal line of Popiel; that the young Poles who graduate from these schools never know war and will be able to work in peace for the good of their homeland; that history work out for them in a less strange way than for previous generations!

Poland is located in the center of Europe. This is why the fulfillment of these wishes is not only in the interest of the Poles, but in the interest of all people of good will on the earth.

MARIAN BRANDYS is widely known in Europe as "the John Gunther of Eastern Europe." A native of Lodz, Poland, and a graduate of the University of Warsaw, he is the author of some fourteen books on current affairs. During World War II, he fought the Germans and was eventually arrested by the Gestapo and sent to a prisoner-of-war camp in Germany. Mr. Brandys is married to the famous Polish actress Halina Mikola, and they live with their two teen-age daughters in Warsaw.